Relationships:

An Interpretation of Matthew

by

Edgar Poe Symmes, III

Reid

A gift wrapped in prayers & best wishes

Poe

DORRANCE PUBLISHING CO., INC.
PITTSBURGH, PENNSYLVANIA 15222

ISBN: 978-1-4349-0169-9

Printed in the United States of America

First Printing

For more information or to order additional books, please contact:
Dorrance Publishing Co., Inc.
701 Smithfield Street
Pittsburgh, Pennsylvania 15222
U.S.A.
1-800-788-7654
www.dorrancebookstore.com

In Loving Memory
of
Wesley Symmes McCabe

Ask, and it shall be given to you;
seek and ye shall find;
knock, and the door will be opened unto you.
for everyone who asketh receiveth;
and he that seeketh findeth;
to him that knocketh, it shall be opened.

Matthew 7:7, 8

Prologue

Life is but an effort to understand and to give expression to our relationship with others. All religion is an effort to understand and to give expression to our relationships with God. As people, we are incurably religious, and we want to understand more fully the endless and mysterious relationship between God and the world and between God and us.

This book is not an effort to convince the reader of the validity of Christianity but rather a witness, an insight into basic Christian principles, and an effort to answer those who are asking elementary questions about faith and through faith, how we build lasting relationships. Faith comes from hearing the message, and the message is heard through the word of Christ. The scripture is clear:

> *But be ye doers of the word, and not hearers only, deceiving your own selves. For if any be a hearer of the word, and not a doer, he is like unto a man beholding his natural face in a glass: for he beholdeth himself, and goeth his way, and straight way forgetteth what manner of man he was. But whoso looketh into the perfect law of liberty, and continueth therein, he being not a forgetful hearer, but a doer of the work, this man shall be blessed in his deed.*
> *James 1:22-25*

Though I will elaborate on my interpretations of the Gospel of Matthew, this is only one definition of many. I pray this text will be but a helpful presentation of basic beliefs and practical ways these beliefs express themselves in living relationships.

Do nothing out of selfish ambition or vain conceit, but in humility consider others better than yourselves. Each of you should look not only to your own interests, but also to the interests of others.

Philippians 2:3, 4

Matthew and the Angel

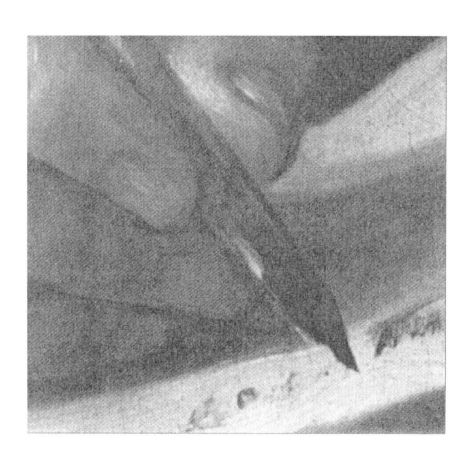

Chapter I

Awesome Responsibility

CHRIST OR NEUTRALITY

He that is not with me is against me; and he that gathereth not with me scattereth abroad. Matthew 121:30

Gathering comes from harvesting and tells of those not sharing in gathering the harvest but scattering the grain about and therefore losing it to the wind. Scattering comes from shepherding which tells about not keeping the flock safe by bringing it into the fold but instead, driving it out to the dangers of the forest. In this one piercing sentence Jesus lays down the impossibility of neutrality. In the ongoing battle against evil, there are only two sides: those for Christ or those against Christ, gathering with Christ or scattering with the Evil One. In our lives, there can be no halfway houses; in all things we must chose our sides; abstention from choice, suspended action, is no way out, because the refusal to give one side assistance is in fact the giving of support to the other.

What things can make a relationship seek impossible neutrality? There is the silence of human nature. So many people of today desire only to be left alone. They automatically push away from anything which is disturbing, and even choice becomes a disturbance. There is the cowardice of human nature. We refuse the way of Christ only because we are afraid to take the stand which Christianity demands. And the basic thing that stops us is that thought of what other people will say. The voice of the crowd is louder in our ears

1

than the voice of God. There is the weakness of human nature. People of today would rather have security than risk, and the older they grow the more that is true. A challenge always involves risk; Christ comes to us with a challenge and often we would rather have the comfort of selfish inaction than the risk of action for Christ. "He who is not with me is against me," this presents us with a problem, for both Mark and Luke have a saying which is the very opposite, "He that is not against me is for us." But these may not be as contradictory as they seem. Jesus spoke the second of them when His disciples came and told Him that they had sought to stop a man from casting out demons in His name, because the man was not one of them. Jesus then suggested, "He that is not with me is against me." This is a test that ought to apply to ourselves. Ask yourself the question: Am I truly on the Lord's side, or, am I trying to shuffle through life in a state of cowardly neutrality? "He that is not against us is for us" This is a test that we ought to apply to others. Am I limiting the Kingdom of God by condemning everyone who does not speak my theology and worship with my liturgy and share my ideas? The saying in Matthew's passage is a test to apply to ourselves, and the saying in Mark and Luke is a test to apply to others. We must first judge ourselves with sternness and others with tolerance.

RESPONSIBILITY OF WORDS

> *O generation of vipers, how can ye, being evil, speak good things? For out of the abundance of the heart the mouth speaketh. A good man out of the good treasure of the heart bringeth forth good things: and an evil man out of the evil treasure bringeth forth evil things. But I say unto you, that every idle word that men shall speak, they shall give account thereof in the day of judgment. For by thy words thou shalt be justified, and by thy words thou shall be condemned.*
>
> **Matthew 12:34-37**

Jesus chooses to speak about the awful responsibility of words. It is here that the Scribes and Pharisees had just spoken the most terrible words. They had looked upon Jesus, the Son of God, and called Him the ally of the Evil One. These words were dreadful words indeed. As a result, Jesus proclaimed that the state of one's heart can be seen through the words one speaks. Years ago, Menander, the Greek dramatist, said: "A man's character can be known from his words." That which is in the heart can come to the surface only through the lips; one can produce through their lips only what they have in their heart. There is nothing so revealing as words. We do not need to talk to one long to determine if a mind is wholesome or dirty; we do not need to listen long to determine if one is kind or cruel; and we do not need to listen long to one who is preaching, teaching, or lecturing to find out whether their mind is clear or whether it is foggy. We are continually revealing what we are by what we say. Jesus said that one would especially render account for their idle words. The Greek word for idle is aergos; ergon is the Greek for a deed; and the prefix a-means without. Aergos described that which was not meant to produce anything. Jesus was saying something which is profoundly true.

It is the words which one speaks without thinking, the words which one utters when the conventional restraints are removed, which really show what one is like. When one is consciously on one's guard, one will be careful what one says and how one says it; but when one is off one's guard, one's words reveal one's character. It is quite possible for one's public words to be fine and noble, and for one's private conversation to be coarse and salacious. In public, they carefully choose what they say; in private they take the sentinels away, and any word leaves the gateway of their lips. So it is with anger; one will say in anger what one really thinks and what one has often wanted to say, but which the cool control of prudence has kept one from saying. Many a person is model of charm and courtesy in public, when they know they are being watched and are deliberately careful about their words; while in their own homes they are dreadful examples of irritability, sarcasm, temper, criticism, and querulous complaint because there is no one to hear and to see. It is a humbling thing and a reminder that the words which show what we are, are the words we speak when our guard is down.

It is often these words which cause the greatest damage. People may say in anger things they would never had said if they were in control of themselves. They may say afterwards that they never meant what they said, but that does not free them from the responsibility of having said it, and the fact that they had said it often leaves a wound that nothing will cure and builds a barrier that nothing will take away. They may say in a relaxed moment a coarse and questionable thing that they would never have said in public and that very thing may lodge in someone's memory and stay there unforgotten. Pythagoras, the Greek philosopher, said "Choose rather to fling a chance stone than to speak a chance word." Once a hurting word is spoken, nothing will bring it back, and it pursues a course of damage wherever it goes. Examine yourselves. Examine your words that you may discover the state of your heart. God does not judge you by words spoken with care and deliberation but by the words spoken when the conventional restraints are gone and the real feelings of your heart come to the surface.

LOOK AGAIN AND CONSECRATE

> *If God so clothes the grass of the field…, shall He not much more clothe you…?*
>
> **Matthew 6:30**

How can we maintain the simplicity of Jesus so that we may understand Him? By receiving His Spirit, recognizing and relying on Him, and obeying Him as He brings us the truth of His Word, life will become amazingly simple. Jesus asks us to consider that "if God so clothes the grass of the field…" how *much more* will He clothe you, if you keep your relationship right with Him? Every time we lose ground in our fellowship with God, it is because we have disrespectfully thought that we knew better than Christ. We allow the cares of this world to enter in, while forgetting the *much more* of our heavenly Father.

Look at the birds of the air, their function is to obey the instincts God placed within them, and God watches over them. Jesus said that if you have the right relationship with Him and will obey His Spirit within you, then God will care for our feathers too.

Consider the lilies of the field. They grow where they are planted. Many of us refuse to grow where God plants us. Therefore, we don't take root anywhere. Jesus said if we would obey the life of God within us, He would look after all other things. If we are not experiencing more, it is because we are not obeying the life God has given us and have cluttered our minds with confusing thoughts and worries. How much time have we wasted asking God senseless questions while we should be absolutely free to concentrate on our service to Him? Consecration is the act of continually separating ourselves from everything except that which God has appointed us to do. It is not a one time experience but an ongoing process. Continually separate yourself and look to God every day of your life.

DO IT NOW

> *Agree with thine adversary quickly*
>
> **Matthew 5:25**

Jesus Christ laid down a very important principle by saying, "Do what you know you must do, now. Do it quickly. If you don't, an inevitable process will begin to work till you have paid the last penny in pain, agony, and distress." God's laws are unchangeable and there is no escape from them. The teachings of Jesus always penetrate right to the heart of our being.

Wanting to make sure that your adversary gives you all your rights is a natural thing. But Jesus says that it is a matter of inescapable and eternal importance to us that we pay our adversary what we owe him. From our Lord's standpoint it doesn't matter whether we are cheated or not, but what does matter is that we don't cheat someone else. Am I insisting on having my own rights, or am I paying what I owe from Jesus Christ's standpoint?

Do it quickly; bring yourself to judgment now. In moral and spiritual matters, you must act immediately. If you don't, the inevitable, relentless process will begin to work. God is determined to have His child as pure, clean, and white as driven snow, and as long as there is disobedience in any point of His teaching, He will allow His Spirit to use whatever process it may take to bring us to obedience. The fact that we insist on proving that we are right is almost always a clear indication that we have some point of disobedience. No wonder the Spirit of God so strongly urges us to stay steadfastly in the light!

Agree with your adversary quickly. Have you suddenly reached a certain place in your relationship with someone, only to find that you have anger in your heart? Confess it quickly; make it right before God. Be reconciled to that person; do it now!

Chapter II

Common Experience

TRUE FRIENDSHIP

> *While he yet talked to the people, behold, his mother and his brethren stood without, desiring to speak with him. Then one said unto him, behold, thy mother and thy brethren stand without, desiring to speak with thee. But he answered and said unto him that told him, who is my mother? And who are my brethren? And he stretched forth his hand toward His disciples, and said, behold my mother and my brethren! For whosoever shall do the will of my Father which is in heaven, the same is my brother, and sister, and mother.*
>
> **Matthew 12:46-50**

One of the great human tragedies of Jesus' life was that those dearest to Him never understood Him. John says, "For even His brothers did not believe in Him." Mark tells us that when Jesus set out on His public mission, His friends tried to restrain Him, for they said He was mad. They thought He was throwing His life away in a kind of insanity.

It was often that when one embarks on the way of Jesus Christ, those dearest could not understand him and were even hostile to him. It has been said by early martyrs that, "A Christian's only relatives are the Saints." Many of our early Quakers had this experience. How many have resented our "fanatical spirit" and thus drove us away?

True friendship and true love are founded on certain things without which they cannot exist. Friendship is founded on a common ideal. People who are very different in their backgrounds, their mental states, and even their methods, can be firm friends, if they have a common ideal for which they work and toward which they strive.

Friendship is founded on a common experience and on the memories which come from that experience. It is when two people have together passed through some great experience and when they can together look back on it, that real friendship begins.

True love is founded on obedience. Jesus said, "You are my friends if you do what I command you." There is no way of showing the reality of love unless by the spirit of obedience.

For all these reasons true friendship is not always a matter of a flesh and blood relationship. It remains true that blood is a tie that nothing can break and that many find their delight and peace in the circle of their family. But it is also true that sometimes one's closest are the people that understand least and that true fellowship is found with those who work for a common ideal and who share a common experience. This certainly is true, even if Christians find that those who should be closest to them are those who are most out of sympathy with them, there remains for them the fellowship of Jesus Christ and the friendship of all who love the Lord.

JUDGMENT'S TIME

Another parable put he forth unto them, saying, the kingdom of heaven is likened unto a man which sowed good seed in his field; but while men slept, his enemy came and sowed tares among the wheat, and went his way. But when the blade was sprung up, and brought forth fruit, then appeared the tares also. So the servants of the householder came and said unto him, Sir, didst not thou sow good seed in thy field? From whence then hath tares? He said unto them, an enemy hath done this. The servants said unto him, wilt thou then that we go and gather them up? But he said, Nay; lest while ye gather up the tares, ye root up also the wheat with them. Let both grow together until the harvest; and in the time of harvest I will say to the reapers, Gather ye together first the tares, and bind them in bundles to burn them: but gather the wheat into my barn. Then Jesus sent the multitude away, and went into the house: and his disciples came unto him, saying, declare unto us the parable of the tares of the field. He answered and said unto them, he that soweth the good seed is the Son of man; the field is the World; the good seed are the children of the kingdom; but the tares are the children of the wicked. One; the enemy that sowed them is the devil; the harvest is the end of the world; and the reapers are the angels. As therefore the tares are gathered and burned in the fire; so shall it be in the end of this world. The son of man shall send forth his angels, and they shall gather out of his kingdom all things that offend, and them which do iniquity; and shall cast them into a furnace of fire: there shall be wailing and gnashing of teeth. Then shall the righteous shine forth as the sun in the kingdom of their Father. Who hath ears to hear, let him hear.

Matthew 13:24-30, 36-43

These practical parables teach us there is always a hostile power in the world, seeking and waiting to destroy the good seed. Our experience is that both kinds of influence act upon our lives, the influence which helps the seed of the world to flourish and to grow and the influence which seeks to destroy the good seed before it can produce fruit at all. The lesson is that we must be forever on our guard.

This parable also says to us how hard it is to distinguish between those who are in the Kingdom and those who are not. One may appear to be good and may in fact be bad; and one may appear to be bad and may yet be good. We are much too quick to classify people and label them good or bad without knowing all the facts.

The parable teaches us not to be so quick with our judgments. If the reapers had had their way, they would have tried to tear out the darnel and they would have torn out the wheat as well. Judgment had to wait until the harvest came. In the end we will be judged, not by any single act or stage in our lives, but by our whole lives. Judgment cannot come until the end. One may make a great mistake, and then redeem oneself and, by the grace of God, atone for it by making the rest of life a lovely event. One may live an honorable life and then in the end wreck it all by a sudden collapse into sin. No one who sees only part of a life can judge the whole; and no one who knows only part of one's life can judge the whole person.

Judgment does come in the end. Judgment is not hasty, but judgment comes. It may be that, humanly speaking, in this life the sinner seems to escape the consequences, but there is a life to come. It may be that, humanly speaking, goodness never seems to enter into its reward, but there is a new world to redress the balance of the old.

The only person with the right to judge is God. It is God alone who can discern the good and the bad; it is God alone who sees all of a person and all of their life. It is God alone who can judge. So, then, ultimately this parable is two things, it is a warning not to judge people at all, and it is a warning that in the end there comes the judgment of God.

TAKING THE INITIATIVE AGAISNT DESPAIR

Rise, let us be going. Matthew 26:46

In the Garden of Gethsemane, the disciples went to sleep when they should have stayed awake, and once they realized what they had done it produced despair. The sense of having done something irreversible tends to make us despair. We say, "Well, it's all over and ruined now; what's the point in trying anymore?" If we think this kind of despair is an exception, we are mistaken. It is a very ordinary human experience. Whenever we realize we have not taken advantage of a magnificent opportunity, we are apt to sink into despair. But Jesus comes and lovingly says to us, in essence, "Sleep on now. That opportunity is lost forever and you can't change that. But get up, and let's go on to the next thing." Let the past sleep, but let it sleep in the sweet embrace of Christ, and let us go on into the invincible future with Him.

There will be experiences like this in all of our lives. We will have times of despair caused by real events in our lives, and we will be unable to lift ourselves out of them. The disciples, in this instance, had done a downright unthinkable thing; they had gone to sleep instead of watching with Jesus. But our Lord came to them, taking the spiritual initiative against their despair, and said, in effect, "Get up, and do the next thing." If we are inspired by God, what is the next thing? It is to trust Him absolutely and to pray on the basis of his redemption.

Never let the senses of past failure defeat your next step.

OUR CAREFUL UNBELIEF

Take no thought for your life, what ye shall eat, or what ye shall drink; nor get for your body, what ye shall put on. Matthew 6:25

Jesus summed up commonsense carefulness in the life of a disciple as unbelief. If we have received the Spirit of God, he will squeeze right through our lives, as if to ask, "Now where do I come into this relationship, this vacation you have planned, or these new books you want to read?" And He always presses the point until we learn to make Him our first consideration. Whenever we put other things first, there is confusion.

"...do not worry about your life." Don't take the pressure of your provision upon yourself. It is not only wrong to worry, it is unbelief; worrying means we do not believe that God can look after the practical details that worry us. Have you ever noticed what Jesus said would choke the Word He put in us? Is it the devil? No, it is the cares of this world." It is always our little worries. We say, "I will not trust when I cannot see," and that is where unbelief begins. The only cure for unbelief is obedience to the Spirit.

The greatest word of Jesus to His disciples is abandon.

THE PATH THROUGH SPIRITUAL CONFUSION

Jesus answered and said, "Ye know not what ye ask."
Matthew 20:22

There are times in our spiritual lives when there is confusion, and the way out of it is not simply to say that you should not be confused. It is not a matter of right and wrong but a matter of God taking us through a way that we temporarily do not understand. And it is only by going through the spiritual confusion that we will come to the understanding of what God wants for us.

Jesus gave the illustration here of a man who appears not to care for his friend. He was saying, in effect, that is how the heavenly Father will appear to you at times. You will think that he is an unkind friend, but remember, He is not. The time will come when everything will be explained. There seems to be a cloud on the friendship of the heart, and often even love itself has to wait in pain and tears for the blessing of fuller fellowship and oneness. When God appears to be completely shrouded, will you hang on with confidence in Him.

Jesus said there are times when your Father will appear as if he were an unnatural father, as if He were callous and indifferent, but remember, he is not. Everyone who asks receives. If all you see is a shadow on the face of the Father right now, hang on to the fact that He will ultimately give you clear understanding and will fully justify Himself in everything that He has allowed into your life.

When the Son of man comes, will He really find faith on the earth? Will He find the kind of faith that counts on Him in spite of the confusion? Stand firm in faith, believing that what Jesus said is true, although in the meantime you do not understand what God is doing. He has bigger issues at stake than the particular things you are asking of Him right now.

Chapter III

Character

FALLING AND RECOVERING

> *And Peter answered him and said, Lord, if it be thou, bid me come unto thee on the water. And he said, Come. And when Peter was come down out of the ship, he walked on the water, To go to Jesus. But when he saw the wind boisterous, he was afraid; and beginning to sink, he cried, saying, Lord, save me. And immediately Jesus stretched forth his hand, and caught him, and said unto him, O thou of little faith, wherefore didst thou doubt? And when they were Come into the ship, the wind ceased. Then they that were in the ship came and worshipped him, saying, of a truth thou are the Son of God.*
>
> **Matthew 14:28-33**

I believe this passage truly reveals the true character of Peter. As in our relationship, Peter was always acting upon impulse and without thinking of what he was doing. It was his mistake that again and again he acted without fully facing the situation and without counting the cost. He was to do exactly the same when he affirmed undying and unshakable loyalty to Jesus and then denied his Lord's name. And yet there are worse sins than that, because Peter's whole trouble was that he was ruled by his heart; however he might sometimes fail, his heart was always in the right place and the instinct of his heart was always love.

Because Peter acted on impulse, he often failed and came to grief. It was always Jesus' insistence that one should look at a situation in all its bleak grimness before one acts. Jesus was completely honest with men; He always made them see how difficult it was to follow Him before they set out upon the Christian way. A great deal of Christian failure is due to acting upon an emotional moment without counting the cost.

But Peter never finally failed, for always in the moment of his failure he clutched at Christ. The wonderful thing about him is that every time he fell, he rose again, and it must have been true that even his failures brought him closer to Jesus Christ. It has been said, a saint is not one who never fails; a saint is one who gets up and goes on again every time they fall. Peter's failure only made him love Jesus more.

These verses finish with another permanent truth. When Jesus got into the boat, the wind sank. The great truth is that, wherever Jesus Christ is, the wildest storm becomes calm. In every kind of storm and stress, the presence of Jesus and the love which flows from the Cross bring peace and serenity and calm.

THE PURE HEART

> *Jesus called the multitude and said to them: "Hear and understand. It is not that which goeth into the mouth which defiles a man; but what cometh out of the mouth that defiles a man. "Then His disciples came to Him and said, "Do you know that when the Pharisees heard your saying, they were shocked by it?" He answered: "Every plant which my heavenly Father did not plant will be rooted up. Let them be. They are blind guides. If the blind lead the blind, both of them will fall into the ditch." Peter said to Him, "Tell us what this dark saying means." He said, "Are you even yet without understanding? Do you not know that everything which goes into a man's mouth goes down into the stomach, and is evacuated out into the drain? But that which comes out of the mouth comes from the heart, and it is these things which defile a man. For from the heart come pernicious thoughts, acts of murder, adultery, theft, false witness, slander. It is these things which defile a man. To eat with unwashed hands does not defile a man."*
>
> **Matthew 15:10-20**

The Scribes and Pharisees where shocked that the very relationship of their religion was cut from beneath their feet. This statement was not only alarming, it was revolutionary. If Jesus was right, their whole theory of religion was wrong. They identified religion and pleasing God with the observing of rules and regulations which had to do with cleanness and with uncleanness, with what one ate and with how one washed their hands before they ate. Jesus identified religion with the state of one's heart and said bluntly that these Pharisaic and Scribal regulations had nothing to do with religion. Jesus said that the Pharisees were blind guides who had no idea of the way to God, and that, if people followed them, all they could expect was to stray off the road and fall into the ditch. And Jesus was profoundly right.

If religion consists in external regulations and observances it is two things. It is far too easy. It is very much easier to abstain from certain foods and to wash the hands in a certain way than it is to love the unlovely and the unlovable and to help the needy at the cost of one's own time, money, comfort, and pleasure. We have still not fully learned this lesson. To go to church regularly, to give liberally to the church, to be a member of a Bible-reading class are all external things. They are means towards religion, but they are not religion. We can not remind ourselves too often that religion consists in personal relationships and in an attitude to God and our fellow man.

Further, if religion consists in external observances, it is quite misleading. Many a person has a faultless life in externals but has the bitterest and the most evil thoughts within their heart. The teaching of Jesus is that not all the outward observances in the world can atone for a heart where pride and bitterness and lust hold sway. It is Jesus teaching that the part of a person that matters is his heart. "Blessed are the poor in heart, for they shall see God." What matters to God is not so much how we act, but why we act; not so much what we actually do, but what we wish in our heart to do. We can see the deed, but God can see the intention.

It is Jesus' teaching and it is a teaching which condemns every one of us that no one can call himself good because he or she observes external rules and regulations; they can call themselves good only when their hearts are pure. The very fact is the end of pride and the reason why every one of us can say only, God be merciful to us sinners.

DISCIPLINE OF HEARING

> *What I tell you in darkness, speak in the light; and what you hear in the ear, preach upon the housetops.*
> **Matthew 10:27**

Sometimes God puts us through the experience and discipline of darkness to teach us to hear and obey Him. Song birds are taught to sing in the dark, and God puts us into the shadow of His hand until we learn to hear Him. Pay attention when God puts you into darkness, and keep your mouth closed while you are there. If you are in the dark now, remain quiet. If you open your mouth in the dark, you will speak while in the wrong mood; darkness is the time to listen. Don't talk to other people about it, don't read books to find out the reason for the darkness, just listen and obey. If you talk to other people, you cannot hear what God is saying. When you are in the dark, listen, and God will give you a very precious message for someone else once you are back in the light.

After every time of darkness, we should experience a mixture of delight and humiliation. If there is only delight, I question whether we have really heard God at all. We should experience delight for having heard God speak but mostly humiliation for having taken so long to hear Him. He will remind you how slow you have been to listen and understand what God has been telling you. And yet God has been saying it for days and even weeks or months. But once we hear Him, He gives us the gift of humiliation, which brings a softness of heart, a gift that will always cause us to listen to God now.

INEVITABLE PENALTY

> *Thou shalt by no means come out thence, till thou hast paid the uttermost farthing.*
>
> **Matthew 5:26**

God is determined to make you pure, holy, and right, and He will not allow you to escape from the scrutiny of the Holy Spirit for even one moment. He urged you to come to judgment immediately when He convicted you, but you did not obey. Then the inevitable process began to work, bringing its inevitable penalty. Now you have been thrown into prison, and you will by no means get out of there till you have paid the last penny.

Yet you ask, "Is this a God of mercy and love?" When seen from God's perspective, it is a glorious ministry of love. God is going to bring you out pure, spotless, and undefiled, but he wants you to recognize the nature you were exhibiting, the nature of demanding your right to yourself. The moment you are willing for God to change your nature, His recreating forces will begin to work. And the moment you realize that God's purpose is to get you into the right relationship with Himself and then with others, He will reach to the very limits of the universe to help you take the right road.

Decide to do it right now, saying, "Yes, Lord, I will write that letter" or, "I will be reconciled to that person now."

These sermons of Jesus are meant for your will and your conscience, not for your head. If you dispute these verses from the Sermon on the Mount with your head, you will dull the appeal to your heart.

If you find yourself asking, "I wonder why I'm not growing spiritually with God." Then ask yourself if you are paying your debts from God's standpoint. Do now what you will have to do someday. Every moral question or call comes with an "ought" behind it, the knowledge of knowing what we ought to do.

GOING THE EXTRA MILE

> *I tell you not to resist an evil person. But whoever slaps you*
> *on your right cheek, turn the other to him also.*
> **Matthew 5:39**

This verse reveals the humiliation of being a Christian. In the natural realm, if a person does not hit back, it is because he is a coward. But in the spiritual realm, it is the very evidence of the Son of God in him if he does not hit back. When you are insulted, you must not only not resent it, but you must make it an opportunity to exhibit the Son of God in your life. And you cannot imitate the nature of Jesus; it is either in you or it is not. A personal insult becomes an opportunity for a saint to reveal the incredible sweetness of the Lord Jesus.

The teaching of the Sermon on the Mount is not, do your duty, but is, in effect, do what is not your duty. It is not your duty to go the second mile or to turn the other cheek, but Jesus said that if we are His disciples, we will always do these things. We will not say, "Oh well, I just can't do any more, and I've been so misrepresented and misunderstood." Every time I insist on having my own rights, I hurt the Son of God, while in fact I can prevent Jesus from being hurt if I will take the blow myself. That is the real meaning of filling up in my flesh what is lacking in the afflictions of Christ. A disciple realizes that it is his Lord's honor that is at stake in his life, not his own honor.

Never look for righteousness in the other person, but never cease to be righteous yourself. We are always looking for justice, yet the essences of the teaching of the Sermon on the Mount is, never look for justice, but never cease to give it.

INDIVIDUALITY

> *Jesus said to His disciples, 'If anyone desires to come after me, let him deny himself.*
>
> **Matthew 16:24.**

Individuality is the hard outer layer surrounding the inner spiritual life. Individuality shoves others aside, separating and isolating people. We see it as the primary characteristic of a child, and rightly so. When we confuse individuality with the spiritual life, we remain isolated. This shell of individuality is God's created natural covering designed to protect the spiritual life. But our individuality must be yielded to God so that our spiritual life may be brought forth into fellowship with Him. Individuality counterfeits spirituality, just as lust counterfeits love. God designed human nature for Himself, but individuality corrupts that human nature for its own purposes.

The characteristics of individuality are independence and self-will. We hinder our spiritual growth more by continually asserting our individuality than any other way. If you say, "I can't believe," it is because your individuality is blocking the way; individuality can never believe. But our spirit cannot help believing. Watch yourself closely when the Spirit of God is at work in you. He pushes you to the limits of your individuality where a choice must be made. The choice is either to say, "I will not surrender," or to surrender, breaking the hard shell of individuality, which allows the spiritual life to emerge. The Holy Spirit narrows it down every time to one thing. It is your individuality that refuses to be reconciled to your brother. God wants to bring you into union with Himself, but unless you are willing to give up your right to yourself, He cannot. Deny your independent right to yourself. Then the real life, the spiritual life is allowed the opportunity to grow.

Chapter IV

The Challenge

BURDEN OF SACRIFICE

> *Then said Jesus unto his disciples, if any man will come after me, let him deny himself, and take up his cross, and follow me. For whosoever will save his life shall lose it: and whosoever will lose his life for my sake shall find it. For what is a man profited, if he shall gain the whole world, and lose his own soul? Or what shall a man give in exchange for his soul?*
>
> **Matthew 16:24-26**

There are particular things Jesus says to us again and again. He confronts us with the challenge of the Christian life. There are things we must be prepared to do, if we are to live the Christian life. We must deny ourselves. Ordinarily we use the word self-denial maybe a week when we do without certain pleasures or luxuries in order to contribute to some good cause. But that is only a very small part of what Jesus meant by self-denial. To deny oneself means in every moment of life to say no to self and yes to God. To deny oneself means once, finally, and for all to dethrone self and to enthrone God. To deny oneself means to obliterate self as the dominant principle of life and to make God the ruling principle, more, the ruling passion, of life. The life of constant self-denial is the life of constant assent to God.

We must take up our cross. That is to say, we must take up the burden of sacrifice. The Christian life is the life of sacrificial service. The Christian may have to abandon personal ambition to serve Christ; it may be that they will discover that the place where they can render the greatest service to Jesus Christ is somewhere where the reward will be small and the prestige non-existent. They will certainly have to sacrifice time, leisure, and pleasure in order to serve God through the service of their fellow man.

To put it quite simply, the comfort of the fireside, the pleasure of a visit to a place of entertainment, may well have to be sacrificed for the duties of the eldership, the calls of the youth, and the visit to the home of some sad or lonely soul. They may well have to sacrifice certain things they could well afford to possess in order to give more away. The Christian life is the sacrificial life.

Luke adds a glowing insight, adds one word to this command of Jesus: "Let him take up his cross daily." The really important thing is not the great moments of sacrifice, but a life lived in the constant hourly awareness of the demands of God and the need of others. The Christian life is a life which is always concerned with others more than it is concerned with itself.

We must follow Jesus Christ. That is to say, we must render to Jesus Christ a perfect obedience. When we were young we used to play a game called "Follow the Leader." Everything the leader did, however difficult, and, in the case of the game, however ridiculous, we had to copy. The Christian life is a constant following of our leader, a constant obedience in thought, word, and action to Jesus Christ. The Christian walks in the footsteps of Christ, wherever He may lead.

There is all the difference in the world between existing and living. To exist is simply to have the lungs breathing and the heart beating; to live is to be alive in a world where everything is worth while, where there is peace in the soul, joy in the heart, and a thrill in every moment. Jesus gives us the recipe for life as distinct from existence.

The one who plays for safety loses life. One who is faithful may die but they die to live; the one who abandons their faith for safety may live, but they live to die. In our day and generation it is not likely to be a question of martyrdom, but it still remains a fact that, if we meet life in the constant search for safety, security, ease, and comfort, if every decision is taken from worldly-wise and prudential motives, we are losing all that makes life worth while. Life becomes a soft and weak thing, when it might have been an adventure. Life becomes a selfish thing, when it might have been radiant with service. Life becomes an earthbound thing, when it might have been reaching for the stars. I once saw a bitter epitaph on a man: "He was born a man and died a florist." The person who plays for safety ceases to be, for we are made in the image of God.

The one who risks all and maybe looks as if they had lost all for Christ finds life. It is the simple lesson of history that it has always been the adventurous souls, bidding farewell to security and safety, which wrote their names on history and greatly helped the world. Unless there had been those prepared to take risks, many a medical cure would not exist. Unless there had been those prepared to take risks, many of the machines which make life easier would never have been invented. Unless there were mothers prepared to take risks, no child would ever be born. It is the one who is prepared "to bet their life that there is a God" who in the end finds life.

Jesus warned: "Suppose a man plays for safety; suppose he gains the whole world; then suppose that he finds that life is not worth living, what can he give to get life back again?" And the truth is that they cannot get life back again. In every decision of life we are doing something to ourselves; we are making ourselves a certain kind of person; we are building up steadily and inevitably a certain kind of character; we are making ourselves able to do certain things and quite unable to do others. It is perfectly possible for one to gain all the things he set his heart upon, and then to awaken one morning to find he missed the most important things of all.

The world stands for material things as opposed to God; and of all material things there are some points to mention. No one can take things with them at the end; they can take only themselves; and if they degraded themselves in order to get things, their regret will be bitter. They cannot help one in the shattering days of life. Material things will never mend a broken heart or cheer a lonely soul. If by any chance they gained their material possessions in a way that is dishonorable, there will come a day when conscience will speak, and they will know hell on this side of the grave.

The world is full of voices crying out that they are fools who sell true life for material things. Jesus asks: "What will a man give in exchange for his soul?" The Greeks say there is no price which will buy a faithful friend or a disciplined soul. Therefore, this final saying of Jesus can mean two things. It can mean once someone has lost his true life, because of his desire for security and for material things, there is no price he can pay to get it back again. He has done something to himself which cannot ever be fully obliterated. It can also mean that someone owes himself and everything else to Jesus Christ; and there is nothing that one can give to Christ in place of his life. It is quite possible for one to try to give his money to Christ and to withhold his life. It is still more possible for one to give lip-service to Christ and to withhold his life. Many a person gives their weekly offering to the Church, but does not attend; obviously that does not satisfy the demands of church membership. The only possible gift to the Church is ourselves, and the only possible gift to Christ is our whole life. There is no substitute for it. Nothing less will do.

WITHIN A CHILD

> *At the same time came the disciples unto Jesus, saying, Who is the greatest in the kingdom of heaven? And Jesus called a little child unto him, and set him in the midst of them, and said, verily I say unto you, except ye be converted, and become as little children, ye shall not enter into the kingdom of heaven. Whosoever therefore shall humble himself as this little child, the same is greatest in the kingdom of heaven.*
>
> **Matthew 18:1-4.**

The disciples asked who was the greatest in the Kingdom of Heaven. Jesus took a child and said that unless they turned and became as this little child, they would not get into the Kingdom at all.

The question of the disciples was: "Who will be the greatest in the Kingdom of Heaven?" The very fact that they asked that question showed that they had no idea at all what the Kingdom of Heaven was. Jesus said, "unless you turn." Jesus was warning them that they were going in completely the wrong direction, away from the Kingdom of Heaven and not towards it. In life it is all a question of what one is aiming at. If they are aiming at the fulfillment of personal ambition, the acquisition of personal power, the enjoyment of personal prestige, the exaltation of self, they are aiming at precisely the opposite of the Kingdom of Heaven. For to be a citizen of the Kingdom means the complete forgetting of self, the obliteration of self, the spending of self in a life which aims at service and not at power. So long as one considers his own self as the most important thing in the world, his back is turned to the Kingdom; if he wants to reach the Kingdom, he must turn around and face the opposite direction.

Jesus took a child. Stories say the child grew to be Ignatius of Antioch, who in later days became a great servant of the church, a great writer, and finally a martyr for Christ. Ignatius was surnamed Theophoros, which means "God-carried," and the story is told that he grew up to learn he had received that name because Jesus carried him on His knee. The story could be so. Maybe it is more likely that it was Peter who asked the question and that it was Peter's little boy whom Jesus took and set in the midst, because we know that Peter was married.

LOOK AGAIN AND THINK

Do not worry about your life. **Matthew 6:25**

The cares of this world, the deceitfulness of riches, and the lust for other things will choke out the life of God in us. We are never free from the recurring waves of this invasion. If the frontline of attack is not about clothes and food, it may be about money or the lack of money, or friends or lack of friends, or the line may be drawn over difficult circumstances. It is one steady invasion, and these things will come in like a flood, unless we allow the Spirit of God to rise up the banner against it.

Our Lord says to be careful only about one thing, our relationship to Him. But our common sense says, "That is absurd, I must consider how I am going to live, and I must consider what I am going to eat and drink." Jesus says you must not. Beware of allowing yourself to think that He says this while not understanding your circumstances. Jesus Christ knows our circumstances better than we do, and He says we must not think about these things to the point where they become the primary concern of our lives. Whenever there are competing concerns in your life, be sure you always put your relationship to God first.

"Sufficient for the day is its own trouble." Jesus tells us not to worry about any troubles or threats today. Look again and think. Keep your mind focused on your heavenly Father.

COME TO ME

Come to Me. Matthew 11:28

The questions that truly matter in life are remarkably few, and they are all answered by these words: "Come to Me." Our Lord's words are not, "Do this, or don't do that," but, "Come to Me." If we will simply come to Jesus, our real lives will be brought into harmony with our real desires. We will actually cease from sin and will bind the song of the Lord beginning in our lives. Where sin and sorrow stops, the song of the saint starts.

Look at the stubbornness of our hearts. We would rather do anything than this one simple childlike thing: "Come to Me." If you truly want to experience ceasing from sin, you must come to Jesus.

Jesus Christ makes Himself the test to determine your genuineness. Look how He used the word "come." At the most unexpected moments in your life there is this whisper of the Lord—"Come to Me"—and you are immediately drawn to Him. Personal contact with Jesus changes everything. Be foolish enough to come and commit yourself to what He says. The attitude necessary for you to come to Him is one where your will has made the determination to let go of everything and deliberately commit it all to Him.

"And I will give you rest," that is, "I will sustain you, causing you to stand firm." He is not saying, "I will put you to bed, hold your hand, and sing you to sleep." But, in essence, He is saying, "I will get you out of bed; out of your listlessness and exhaustion, and out of your condition of being half dead while you are still alive. I will penetrate you with the spirit of life, and you will be sustained by the perfection of vital activity." Yet we become so weak and pitiful and talk about suffering the will of the Lord. Grab the power of the Son of God.

GLORIOUSLY DIFFICULT

> *Enter by the narrow gate...Because narrow is the gate and difficult is the way which leads to life.*
>
> **Matthew 7:13.**

We must always remember if we are going to live as disciples of Jesus that all efforts of worth and excellence are difficult. The Christian life is gloriously difficult, but its difficulty does not make us faint and cave in; it stirs us up to overcome.

God saves people by His sovereign grace through the atonement of Jesus, and it is God who works in you both to will and to do for His good pleasure. But we must practice that salvation in our everyday, practical living. If we will only start on the basis of His redemption to do what He commands, then we will find that we can do it. If we fail, it is because we have not yet put into practice what God has placed within us. But a crisis will reveal whether or not we have been putting it into practice. If we will obey the Spirit of God and practice in our physical life what God has placed within us by His Spirit, then when a crisis does come we will find that our own natures, as well as the grace of God, will stand by us.

God gives us difficult things to do. His salvation is a joyous thing, but it is also something that requires bravery, courage, and holiness. It tests us for all we are worth. Jesus is bringing many sons to glory, and God will not shield us from the requirements of sonship. God's grace produces men and women with a strong family likeness to Jesus Christ, not pampered, spoiled weaklings. It takes a tremendous amount of discipline to live the worthy and excellent life of a disciple of Jesus in the realities of life. It is always necessary for us to make an effort to live a life of worth and excellence.

Chapter V

Uncommon Ethics

PERSONAL RELATIONSHIPS

Matthew 18:1-35.

Matthew 18 is a very important chapter for Christian ethics because it deals with those qualities which should characterize the personal relationships of the Christian. There are several distinct qualities which should mark the personal relationship of a Christian.

Humility should be considered the foundation. Only the person who has the humility of the child is a citizen of the Kingdom of Heaven. Personal ambition, personal prestige, personal publicity, and personal profits are motives which can find no place in the life of the Christian. The Christian is one who forgets self in his devotion to Jesus Christ and in his service of his fellow man.

Responsibility is a second pillar. The greatest of all sins is to teach another to sin, especially if that other should be a weaker, a younger, and a less experienced person. God's sternest judgment is reserved for those who put a stumbling block in the way of others. Christians are constantly aware that they are responsible for the effects of their lives, their deeds, their words, and their example on other people.

Here follows the quality of self-renunciation. Christians are like athletes for whom no training is too hard, if by it they may win the prize; they are like students who will sacrifice pleasure and leisure to reach the crown.

Christians are ready surgically to cut from life everything which would keep them from rendering a perfect obedience to God.

There is individual care. Christians realize that God cares for them individually, and they must reflect that individual care in their care for others. They never think in terms of crowds; they think in terms of people. For God, no person is unimportant and no one is lost in the crowd; for the Christian every person is important and is a child of God, who, if lost, must be found. The individual care of the Christian is in fact the motive and the dynamic of evangelism.

There is the quality of discipline. Christian kindness and Christian forgiveness do not mean that one who is in error is to be allowed to do as he pleases. Such a person must be guided and corrected and, if need be, disciplined back into the right way. But that discipline is always to be given in humble love and not in self-righteous condemnation. It is always to be given with the desire for reconciliation and never with the desire for vengeance.

There is the quality of fellowship. We might even say that Christians are people who pray together. They are people who in fellowship seek the will of God, who in fellowship listen and worship together. Individualism is the opposite of Christianity.

And there is the spirit of forgiveness. Christians forgiveness of their fellow man is founded on the fact that they themselves are forgiven. He forgives others even as God, for Christ's sake, has forgiven him.

IN MY NAME

> *And who so shall receive one such little child in my name receiveth me. But who so shall offend one of these little ones which believe in me, it were better for him that a millstone were hanged about his neck, and that he were drowned in the depth of the sea. Woe unto the world because of offences! For it must needs be that offences come; but woe to that man by whom the offence cometh! Take heed that ye despise not one of these little ones; for I say unto you, that in heaven their angels do always behold the face of my Father which is in heaven.*
> **Matthew 18:5-7, 10**

It is Matthew's consistent custom to gather together the teaching of Jesus under certain headings; Matthew arranges it systematically. In the early part of this passage he is collecting Jesus' teaching about children, and we must remember that the Jews used the word child in a double sense. They used it

24

literally of the young word child, but regularly a teacher's disciples were called his sons or his children. Therefore, a child also means a beginner in the faith, one who has just begun to believe, one who is not yet mature and established in the faith, one who has just begun on the right way and who may very easily be deflected from it. In this passage very often the child means both the young child and the beginner on the Christian way.

Jesus said that whoever received one little child in His name received Him. The phrase, "in My name," can have a double meaning. It can mean "for My sake." The care of children is something which is carried out for the sake of Jesus Christ. To teach a child, to bring up a child in the way they ought to go, is something which is done not only for the sake of the child, but for the sake of Jesus Himself. It can also mean, "with a blessing." It can mean receiving the child, and, as it were, naming the name of Jesus over him. He who brings Jesus and the blessing of Jesus to a child is doing Christ's work.

To receive the child is also a phrase which is capable of bearing more than one meaning. It can mean, not so much to receive a child, as to receive a person who has this childlike quality of humility. In this highly competitive world it is very easy to pay more attention to the person who is pugnacious, aggressive, self-assertive, and full of self-confidence. It is easy to pay more attention to the person who, in the worldly sense of the term, has made a success of life.

Jesus may well be saying that the most important people are not the runners and those who have climbed to the top of the tree by pushing everyone else out of the way, but the quiet, humble, simple people, who have the heart of a child.

It can mean simply to welcome the child, to give him the care, the love and the teaching which he requires to make him into a good person. To help a child to live well and to know God better is to help Jesus Christ.

But this phrase can have another and very wonderful meaning as well. It can mean to see Christ in the child. To teach unruly, disobedient, restless little children can be a tedious job. To satisfy the physical needs of a child, to wash their clothes, mend their cuts and soothe their bruises, and cook their meals may often seem a very unromantic task—the cooker and the sink do not have much glamour—but there is no one in all this world who helps Jesus Christ more than the teacher of little child and the harassed, hard pressed mother in the home. All will find glory in the night, if in the child they sometimes glimpse none other than Jesus himself.

This passage reflects the terrible weight of responsibility it leaves upon every one of us. It stresses the terror of teaching another to sin. It is true to say that no man sins uninvited; and the bearer of the invitation is often a fellow-man. One must always be confronted with their first temptation to sin;

they must always receive their first encouragement to do the wrong thing; they must always experience their first push along the way to the forbidden things. The Jews took the view that the most unforgivable of all sins is to teach another to sin; and for this reason, a person's own sins can be forgiven, for in a sense they are limited in their consequences; but if we teach another to sin, they in turn may teach still another, and a trail of sin is set in motion with no foreseeable end.

There is nothing in this world more terrible than to destroy someone's innocence. And if one has any conscience left, there is nothing which will haunt them more. The sin of all sins is to teach another to sin. The passage stresses the terror of the punishment of those who teach another to sin. If one teaches another to sin, it would be better for them that a millstone was hung about their neck and they were drowned in the depths of the sea. The very size of a millstone indicates the awfulness of the condemnation.

In the Greek translation, it is said, not so much that one would be better to be drowned in the depths of the sea, but that it would be better if they were drowned far out in the open sea. The Jews feared the sea; for them Heaven was a place where there would be no more sea. The very picture of drowning had its terror for the Jew. Drowning was sometimes a Roman punishment, but never Jewish. To the Jew it was the symbol of utter destruction. When the Rabbis taught that heathen and Gentile objects were to be utterly destroyed they said that they must be "cast into the salt sea."

The passage has a warning to silence all evasion. This is a sin stained world and a tempting world; no one can go out into it without meeting seductions to sin. That is especially so if we go out from a protected home where no evil influence was ever allowed to play upon them. Jesus says, "that is perfectly true; this world is full of temptations; that is inevitable in a world into which sin has entered; but that does not lessen the responsibility of one who is the cause of a stumbling block being placed in the way of a younger person or of a beginner in the faith."

We know that this is a tempting world; it is therefore the Christian's duty to remove stumbling blocks, never to be the cause of putting them in another's way. This means that it is not only a sin to put a stumbling block in another's way; it is also a sin even to bring that person into any situation, circumstance, or environment where they may meet with such a stumbling block. No Christian can be satisfied to live complacently and lethargically in a civilization where there are conditions of living and housing and life in general where a young person has no chance of escaping the seductions of sin.

Subsequently, the passage stresses the supreme importance of the child. "Their angels," said Jesus, "always behold the face of my Father who is in Heaven." In the time of Jesus the Jews had a very highly developed angelology. Every nation had its angel; every natural force, such as the wind and the thunder and the lightning and the rain, had its angel. They even said, very beautifully, that every blade of grass had its angel. So, then, they believed that every child had their guardian angel.

To say that these angels behold the face of God in Heaven meant that they always have the right of direct access to God. In the sight of God, the children are so important that their guardian angels always have the right of direct access to the inner presence of God.

To Christians the great value of a child must always lie in the possibilities which are locked up within them. Everything depends on how they are taught and trained. The possibilities may never be realized; they may be stifled and stunted; that which might be used for good may be deflected to the purposes of evil; or they may be unleashed in such a way that a new tide of power floods the earth.

One of the great warriors and knightly figures of the eleventh century was Duke Robert of Burgundy. He was about to travel to a far away campaign. He had a baby son who was his heir, and, before he departed, he made his barons and nobles come and swear fealty to the little infant, in the event of anything happening to himself. They came with their waving plumes and their clanking armor and knelt before the child. One great baron smiled and Duke Robert asked why he was smiling. He said, "the child is so little." "Yes," said Duke Robert, "he's little but he will grow." Indeed he grew, for that baby became William the Conqueror of England.

In every child there are infinite possibilities for good or ill. It is the supreme responsibility of the parent, of the teacher, of the Christian, to see that their dynamic possibilities for good are realized. To stifle them, to leave them untapped, to twist them into evil powers, is sin.

LIVING SIMPLE AND FOCUSED

> *Look at the birds of the air ….Consider the lilies of the field.*
>   **Matthew 6:26, 28**

Consider the lilies of the field, how they grow; they neither toil nor spin; they simply are. Think of the sea, the air, the sun, the stars, and the moon; all of these simply are as well, yet what a ministry and service they render on our behalf. So often we impair God's designed influence, which He desires to exhibit through us, because of our own conscious efforts to be consistent and useful.

Jesus said there is only one way to develop and grow spiritually, and that is through focusing and concentrating on God. In essence, Jesus was saying, "Do not worry about being of use to others; simply believe on Me." Pay attention to the Source, and out of you will flow rivers of living water. We cannot discover the source of our natural life through common sense and reasoning and Jesus is teaching here that growth in our spiritual life comes not from focusing directly on it, but from concentrating on our Father in heaven. Our heavenly Father knows our circumstances, and if we will stay focused on Him, instead of our circumstances, we will grow spiritually, just as the lilies of the field.

The people who influence us the most are not those who detain us with their continual talk, but those who live their lives like the stars in the sky and the lilies of the field, simply and unaffectedly. These are the lives that mold and shape us.

If you want to be of use to God, maintain the proper relationship with Jesus Christ by staying focused on Him, and He will make use of you every minute you live; yet you will be unaware, on the conscious level of your life, that you are being used of Him.

CRITICIZING OTHERS

Judge not, that ye be not judged. **Matthew 7:1**

Jesus' instructions with regard to judging others are very simply put; He says, "Don't." The average Christian is the most piercingly critical individual known. Criticism is one of the ordinary activities of people, but in the spiritual realm nothing is accomplished by it. The effect of criticism is the dividing up of the strengths of the one being criticized. The Holy Spirit is the only one in the proper position to criticize, and He alone is able to show what is wrong without hurting and wounding. It is impossible to enter into fellowship with God when you are in a critical mood. Criticism serves to make you harsh, vindictive, and cruel and leaves you with the soothing and flattering idea that you are somehow superior to others. Jesus says that as his disciple you should cultivated a temperament that is never critical. This will not happen quickly but must be developed over a span of time. You must constantly beware of anything that causes you to think of yourself as a superior person.

There is no escaping the penetrating search of my life by Jesus. If I see the little speck in your eye, it means that I have a plank of timber in my own. Every wrong thing that I see in you, God finds in me. Every time I judge, I condemn myself. Stop having a measuring stick for other people. There is always at least one more fact, which we know nothing about, in every person's situation. The first thing God does is to give us a thorough spiritual cleaning. After that, there is no possibility of pride remaining in us. I have never met a person I could despair of, or lose all hope for, after discerning what lies in me apart from the grace of God.

DIVINE CONTROL

> *How much more will your Father who is in heaven give*
> *good things to those who ask him.*
> **Matthew 7:11.**

Jesus is laying down the rules of conduct in this passage for those people who have His Spirit. He urges us to keep our minds filled with the concept of God's control over everything, which means that a disciple must maintain an attitude of perfect trust and an eagerness to ask and to seek.

Fill your mind with the thought that God is there. And once your mind is truly filled with that thought, when you experience difficulties it will be as easy as breathing for you to remember, "My heavenly Father knows all about this!" This will be no effort at all, but will be a natural thing for you when difficulties and uncertainties arise. Before you formed this concept of divine control so powerfully in your mind, you used to go from person to person seeking help, but now you go to God about it. Jesus is laying down the rules of conduct for those people who have His Spirit, and it works on the following principle: God is my Father, he loves me, and I will never think of anything that he will forget, so why should I worry.?

Jesus said there are times when God cannot lift the darkness from you, but you should trust Him. At times God will appear like an unkind friend, but He is not; He will appear like an unnatural father, but he is not; He will appear like an unjust judge, but he is not. Keep the thought that the mind of God is behind all things strong and growing. Not even the smallest detail of life happens unless God's will is behind it. Therefore, you can rest in perfect confidence in Him. Prayer is not only asking, but is an attitude of the mind which produces the atmosphere in which asking is perfectly natural. Ask, and it will be given to you.

Chapter VI

Empowering Love

THE PROTECTING LOVE

> *How think ye? If a man have an hundred sheep, and one of them be gone astray, doth he not leave the ninety and nine, and goeth into the mountains, and seeketh that which is gone astray? And if so be that he find it, verily I say unto you, he rejoiceth more of that sheep, than of the ninety and nine which went not astray. Even so it is not the will of your Father which is in heaven, that one of these little ones should perish.*

Matthew 18:12-14

A simple parable. In Judaea it was tragically easy for sheep to go astray. The land on the hill country is confined, therefore, the sheep are ever liable to wander; and, if they stray from the grass of the plateau into the gullies and the ravines at each side, they have every chance of finishing up on some ledge marooned there until they die.

The Palestinian shepherds were experts at tracking down their lost sheep. They could follow their track for miles, and they would brave the cliffs and the precipice to bringing them back. In the time of Jesus the flocks were often communal flocks; they belonged not to an individual, but to a village. Therefore, there were usually two to three shepherds with them. And this is why one could leave the flock to search. It was a rule that, if a sheep could not be brought back alive, then at least, if it was at all possible, its fleece or its bones must be brought back to prove that it was dead.

We can only imagine how the shepherds would return with their flocks to the village at evening time and tell the story of how one of their own was still out on the mountainside seeking a wanderer. We can imagine how the eyes of the people would turn ever and again to the hillside watching for the shepherd who had not come home, and we can imagine the shout of joy when they saw him striding along the pathway with the weary wanderer slung across his shoulder, safe at last. We can imagine how the whole village would welcome him and gather round with gladness to hear the story of the sheep that was lost and now found. I believe that this was Jesus' favorite picture of God and of God's love. Many things are taught through this parable about that love.

It says that the love of God is an individual love. The ninety-nine were not enough; one sheep was out on the hillside and the shepherd could not rest until he had brought it home. However large a family a parent has, he cannot spare even one; there is not one who does not matter. God is like that; God cannot be happy until the last wanderer is gathered in.

God's love is a patient love. Sheep are proverbially foolish creatures. The sheep has no one but itself to blame for the danger it had got itself into. Man is apt to have so little patience with the foolish ones. When they get into trouble, we are apt to say, "It's their own fault; they brought it on themselves; don't waste any sympathy on fools." God is not like that. The sheep might be foolish but the shepherd would still risk his life to save it. We may be fools but God loves even the foolish person who has no one to blame but himself for their sin and their sorrow.

The love of God is rejoicing love. Nothing but joy. There are no recriminations; there is no receiving back with a grudge and a sense of superior contempt; it is all joy. So often we accept one who is penitent with a moral lecture and a clear indication that they must regard themselves as contemptible and the practical statement that we have no further use for them and do not propose to trust them ever again. It is human never to forget a person's past and always to remember their sins against them. But God puts our sins behind his back; and when we return to Him, it is all joy.

God is our protector and the love of God is a protecting love. It is a love which seeks and saves. There can be a love which ruins; there can be a love which softens; but the love of God is a protecting love which saves one for the service of their fellow-man, a love which makes the wanderer wise, the weak strong, the sinner pure, the captive of sin the free person of holiness, and the vanquished by temptation its conqueror.

BROKEN RELATIONSHIPS

> *Moreover if thy brother shall trespass against thee, go and tell him his fault between thee and him alone: if he shall hear thee, thou hast gained thy brother. But if he will not hear thee, then take with thee one or two more, that in the mouth of two or three witnesses every word may be established. And if he shall neglect to hear them, tell it unto the church: But if he neglects to hear the church, let him be unto thee as a heathen man and a publican. Verily I say unto you, what soever ye shall bind on earth shall be bound in heaven: and whatsoever ye shall loose on earth shall be loosed in heaven.*
>
> **Matthew 18:15-18.**

This could be one of the most difficult passages to interpret in the gospel of Matthew. It is difficult because it does not sound true and it does not sound like Jesus; it sounds much more like regulations of an ecclesiastical committee. It is not possible that Jesus said this in its present form. Jesus could not have told His disciples to take things to the Church, for it did not exist; and the passage implies a full developed and organized Church with a system of ecclesiastical discipline. And it speaks of tax collectors and Gentiles as irreclaimable outsiders.

Yet Jesus was accused of being the friend of tax collectors and sinners. He never spoke of them as hopeless outsiders, but always with sympathy and love, and even with praise. He actually said that the tax collectors and harlots will go into the Kingdom before the orthodox religious people of the time. Furthermore, the whole tone of the passage is that there is a limit to forgiveness, that there comes a time when a person may be abandoned as beyond hope, counsel which is impossible to think of Jesus giving. The last verse actually seems to give the Church the power to retain and to forgive sins. There are many reasons to make us think that this, as it stands, cannot be a correct report of the words of Jesus, but an adaptation made by the Church in later days, when Church discipline was rather a thing of rules and regulations than of love and forgiveness.

Although this passage may certainly not be a correct report of what Jesus said, it is equally certain that it goes back to something He did say. Can we walk behind it and come to the actual commandment of Jesus? At its best what Jesus was saying was, "If anyone sins against you, spare no effort to make that man admit his fault, and to get things right again between you and him." It means that we must never tolerate any situation in which there is a

32

breach of personal relationships between us and another member of the Christian community.

Suppose something does go wrong, what are we to do to make it right? With this passage, we are given a whole realm of actions for the mending of broken relationships within the Christian fellowship. If we feel that someone has wronged us, we should immediately put our complaint into words. The worst thing we can do about a wrong is to brood about it. That is fatal. It can poison the whole mind and life, until we can think of nothing else but our sense of personal injury. Any such feeling should be brought out into the open, faced, and stated, and often the very stating of it will show how unimportant and trivial the whole thing is.

If we feel someone has wronged us, we should go to see them personally. More trouble has been caused by the writing of letters than by almost anything else. A letter may be misread and misunderstood; it may quite unconsciously convey a tone it was never meant to convey. If we have a difference with someone, there is only one way to settle it, and that is face to face. The spoken word can often settle a difference which the written word would only have exacerbated.

If a private and personal meeting fails of its purpose, we should take some wise person or persons with us. "A single witness shall not prevail against a man for nay crime or from any wrong it connection with any offense that he has committed; only on the evidence of two witnesses or of three witnesses, shall a charge be sustained." That is the saying which Matthew has in mind. But in this case the taking of the witness is not meant to be a way of proving to a person that they committed an offense. It is meant to help the process of reconciliation. A person often hates those whom they have injured most of all, and it may well be that nothing we can say can win them back. But to talk matters over with some wise, kindly, and gracious person present is to create a new atmosphere in which there is at least a chance that we should see ourselves "as others see us." The Rabbis had a wise saying, "Judge not alone, for none may judge alone save One that is God."

If all this fails, we must take our personal troubles to the Christian fellowship. Why? Because troubles are never settled by going to lawyers or by Christ-less argument. Legalism merely produces further trouble. It is in an atmosphere of Christian prayer, Christian love, and Christian fellowship that personal relationships may be righted. The clear assumption is that the Church fellowship is Christian and seeks to judge everything, not in the light of a book of practice and procedure, but in the light of love.

Matthew says that, if even that does not succeed, then the person who has wronged us is to be regarded as a Gentile and a tax collector. The first impression is that the person ought to be abandoned as hopeless and irreclaimable, but that is precisely what Jesus cannot have meant. He never set limits to human forgiveness. What then could he mean?

Jesus always spoke of tax collectors and sinners with sympathy, gentleness, and an appreciation of their good qualities. Therefore, Jesus said something like this: "When you have done all this, when you have given the sinner every chance, and when he remains stubborn and obdurate, you may think that he is not better than renegade tax collector, or even a godless Gentile. Well, you may be right. But I have not found the tax collectors and the Gentiles hopeless. My experience of them is that they, too, have a heart to be touched; and there are many of them, like Matthew and Zacchaeus, who have become my best friends. Even if the stubborn sinner is like a tax collector or a Gentile, you may still win him, as I have done."

This is the challenge to win a person with the love which can touch even the hardest heart. It is not a statement that some people are hopeless; it is a statement that Jesus Christ has found no person hopeless, and neither must we.

Look at the saying about losing and binding. It is a difficult saying. It cannot mean that the Church can remit or forgive sins and so settle a person's destiny in time or in eternity. What it may well mean is that the relationships which we establish with our fellow men last not only through time but into eternity, therefore, we must get them right.

JESUS' AGONY AND OUR ACCESS

> *Jesus came with them to a place called Gethsemane, and said to the disciples... 'Stay here and watch with Me'.*
> **Matthew 26:36, 38**

We can never fully comprehend Christ's agony in the Garden of Gethsemane, but at least we don't have to misunderstand it. It is the agony of God and man in one Person, coming face to face with sin. We cannot learn about Gethsemane through personal experience. Gethsemane and Calvary represent something totally unique; they are the gateway into life for us all.

It was not death on the cross that Jesus agonized over in Gethsemane. In fact, He stated very emphatically that He came with the purpose of dying. His concern was that He might not get through this struggle as the Son of man. He was confident of getting through it as the Son of God; Satan could not touch Him there.

But Satan's assault was that our Lord would come through for us on His own solely as the Son of Man. If Jesus had done that, He could not have been our Savior. The record of His agony in Gethsemane in light of His earlier wilderness temptation is clear; the devil departed from Him until an opportune time. In Gethsemane, Satan came back and was overthrown again. Satan's final assault against our Lord as the Son of Man was in Gethsemane.

The agony in Gethsemane was the agony of the Son of God in fulfilling His destiny as the Savior of the world. The veil is pulled back here to reveal all that it cost Him to make it possible for us to become sons of God. His agony was the basis for the simplicity of our salvation. The Cross of Christ was a triumph for the Son of Man. It was not only a sign that our Lord had triumphed, but that He had triumphed to save the human race. Because of what the Son of man went through, every human being has been provided with a way of access into the very presence of God.

OUR MOTIVES

> *Unless your righteousness shall exceed the righteousness of the scribes and Pharisees, you shall in no case enter into the kingdom of heaven.*
>
> **Matthew 5:20**

The characteristic of a disciple is not that he does good things, but that he is good in his motives, having been made good by the supernatural grace of God. The only thing that exceeds right-doing is right-being. Christ came to place within anyone who would let Him a new heredity that would have a righteousness exceeding that of the scribes and Pharisees. Jesus is saying, "If you are My disciple, you must be right not only in your actions, but also in your motives, your aspirations, and in the deep recesses of the thoughts of your mind." Your motives must be so pure that God Almighty can see nothing to rebuke. Who can stand in the eternal light of God and have nothing for Him to rebuke? Only the Son of God, and Jesus claims that through His redemption He can place within anyone His own nature and make that person as pure and as simple as a child. The purity God demands is impossible unless we can be remade within, and that is exactly what Jesus has undertaken to do through his redemption.

No one can make himself pure by obeying laws. Jesus does not give us rules and regulations; He gives us His teachings which are truths that can only be interpreted by His nature which He places within us. The great wonder of Jesus Christ's salvation is that He changes our heredity. He does not change human nature; He changes its source, and thereby its motives as well.

TRUTH OF GOD

Jesus answered and said, 'I thank thee, Father...that thou hast hidden these things from the wise and prudent and have revealed them unto babes.'

Matthew 11:25

We do not grow into a spiritual relationship step by step; we either have a relationship or we do not. God does not continue to cleanse us more and more from sin. But if we walk in the light, we are cleansed from all sin. It is a matter of obedience, and once we obey, the relationship is instantly perfected. But if we turn away from obedience for even one second, darkness and death are immediately at work again.

All of God's revealed truths are sealed until they are opened to us through obedience. You will never open them through philosophy or thinking. But once you obey, a flash of light comes immediately. Let God's truth work into you by immersing yourself in it, not by worrying into it. The only way you can get to know the truth of God is to stop trying to find out and by being born again. If you obey God in the first thing He shows you, then He instantly opens up the next truth to you. You could read volumes on the work of the Holy Spirit, when five minutes of total, uncompromising obedience would make things as clear as sunlight. Don't say, "I suppose I will understand these things someday!" You can understand them now. And it is not study that brings understanding to you but obedience. Even the smallest bit of obedience opens heaven, and the deepest truths of God immediately become yours. Yet God will never reveal more truth about Himself to you until you have obeyed what you know already. Beware of becoming one of the wise and prudent. If anyone wills to do His will, he shall know the truth of God.

Chapter VII

Unselfish Unity

EFFECTIVE PRAYER

> *Again I say unto you, that if two of you shall agree on earth as touching any thing that they shall ask, it shall be done for them of my father which is in heaven. For where two or three are gathered together in my name, there am I in the midst of them.*
>
> **Matthew 18:19-20**

This is a saying of Jesus that needs to be investigated or we will be left with heartbreak and great disappointment. Jesus said, if two upon earth agree upon any matter for which they are praying, they will receive it from God. If that is to be taken literally and without any qualification, it is manifestly untrue. Many times two people have agreed to pray for the physical or the spiritual welfare of a loved one, and their prayer has not, in the literal sense, been answered. How many times have God's people agreed to pray for the conversion of their own land or the conversion of the heathen and the coming of the Kingdom, and even yet that prayer is far from being fully answered? People agree to pray and pray desperately and do not receive that for which they pray. There is no point in refusing to face the facts of the situation, and nothing but harm can result from teaching people to expect what does not happen. But there is a precious depth when we see what this saying means.

It means that prayer must never be selfish and that selfish prayer cannot find an answer. We are not meant to pray only for our own needs, thinking of nothing and no one but ourselves; we are meant to pray as members of a fellowship, in agreement, remembering that life and the world are not arranged for us as individuals but for the fellowship as a whole. It would often happen that, if our prayers were answered, the prayers of someone else would be disappointed. Often our prayers for our success would necessarily involve someone else's failure. Effective prayer must be the prayer of agreement, from which the element of selfish concentration on our own needs and desires has been quite cleansed away.

When prayer is unselfish, it is always answered. But here as everywhere we must remember the basic law of prayer; that law is that in prayer we receive, not the answer which we desire, but the answer which God in His wisdom and His love knows to be best. Simply because we are human beings, with human hearts and fears, hopes, and desires, most of our prayers are prayers for escape. We pray to be saved from some trial, some sorrow, some disappointment, and some hurting and difficult situation. And always God's answer is the offer not of escape but of victory. God does not give us escape from a human situation. He enables us to accept what we cannot understand; He enables us to endure what without Him would be unendurable; He enables us to face what without Him would be beyond all facing. The perfect example of all of this is Jesus in Gethsemane. He prayed to be released from the dread situation which confronted Him; He was not released from it, but He was given power to meet it, to endure it, and to conquer it. When we pray unselfishly, God sends His answer, but the answer is always His answer and not necessarily ours.

Jesus continues to say where two or three are gathered in His name, He is there in the midst of them. The Jews themselves had a saying, "Where two sit and are occupied with the study of the Law, the glory of God is among them." We can take this great promise of Jesus into two spheres. We may take it into the sphere of the Church. Jesus is just as much present in the little congregation as in the great mass meeting. He is just as much present at the prayer meeting or the bible study circle with their handful or people as in the crowded stadium. He is not the slave of numbers. He is there wherever faithful hearts meet, however few they may be, for He gives all of Himself to each individual person.

And we may take it into the sphere of the home. One of the earliest interpretations of this saying of Jesus was that the two or three are father, mother, and child, and that it means that Jesus is there, the unseen guest in every home.

There are those who never give of their best except on a great occasion, but for Jesus Christ every occasion where even two or three are gathered in His name is a great occasion.

MARRIAGE AND DIVORCE

> *And it came to pass, that when Jesus had finished these sayings, he departed from Galilee, and came into the coasts of Judaea beyond Jordan; and great multitudes followed him; and he healed them there. The Pharisees also came unto him, tempting him, and saying unto him, is it lawful for a man to put away his wife for every cause? And he answered and said unto them, have ye not read, that he which made them at the beginning made them male and female, and said, for this cause shall a man leave father and mother, and shall cleave to his wife: and they twain shall be one flesh? Wherefore they are no more twain, but one flesh. What therefore God hath joined together, let not man put asunder. They say unto him, why did Moses then command to give a writing of divorcement, and to put her away? He saith unto them, Moses because of the hardness of your hearts suffered you to put away your wives: but from the beginning it was not so. And I say unto you, whosoever shall put away his wife, except it be for fornication, and shall marry another, committeth adultery; and whoso marrieth her which is put away doth commit adultery.*
>
> **Matthew 19:1-9**

In this passage, Jesus is dealing with what was in His day, as it is in our own, a troubled and important question. Divorce was something about which there was no unanimity among the Jews, and the Pharisees were deliberately trying to involve Jesus in controversy.

No nation has ever had a higher view of marriage than the Jews. Marriage was a sacred duty. To remain unmarried after the age of twenty, except in order to concentrate upon the study of the Law, was to break a positive commandment to "be fruitful and multiply." Marriage was not to be entered into carelessly or lightly. The Mosaic teaching was that a man must marry a virgin of good parentage. He must never corrupt another man's wife, and he must not marry a woman who had been a slave or a harlot. If a man accused his wife of not being a virgin when he married her, he must bring proof of his accusation. Her father or brother must defend her. If the girl was vindicated he must take her in marriage and could never again put her away, except for the most flagrant sin. If the accusation was proved to have been reckless and malicious, the man who made it must be beaten with forty stripes save one and must pay fifty shekels to the girl's father. But if the charge was proved and the girl found guilty, if she was one of the ordinary people, the law was that she must be stoned to death, and if she was the daughter of a priest, she must be burned alive.

If a man seduced a girl who was espoused to be married, and the seduction took place with her consent, both he and she must be put to death. If in a lonely place or where there was no help present, the man forced the girl into sin, the man alone was put to death. If a man seduced an unexposed girl, he must marry her, or, if her father was unwilling for him to marry her, he must pay the father fifty shekels.

The Jewish laws of marriage and of purity aimed very high. Ideally, divorce was hated. God had said, "I hate divorce." It was said that the very altar wept tears when a man divorced the wife of his youth.

But ideal and actuality does not go hand in hand. In this situation there were two dangerous and damaging elements. First, in the eyes of the Jewish law a woman was a thing. She was the possession of her father, or of her husband as the case might be, and, therefore, she had, technically, no legal rights at all. Most Jewish marriages were arranged either by the parents or professional match makers. A girl might be engaged to be married in childhood and was often engaged to be married to a man whom she had never seen. There was a safeguard that when she came to the age of twelve she could repudiate her father's choice of husband. But in matters of divorce, the general law was that the initiative must lie with the husband. The law ran: "A woman may be divorced with or without her consent, but a man can be divorced only with his consent." The woman could never initiate the process of divorce; she could not divorce, she had to be divorced.

There were certain safeguards. If a man divorced his wife on any other grounds than those of flagrant immorality, he must return her dowry, and this must have been a barrier to irresponsible divorce. The courts might put pressure on a man to divorce his wife, in the case, for instance, of refusal to consummate the marriage, of impotence, or of proved inability to support her properly. A wife could force her husband to divorce her if he contracted a terrible disease, such as leprosy, or it he was a tanner, which involved the gathering of dog's dung, or if he proposed to make her leave the Holy Land. But, for the most part, the law was that the woman had no legal rights, and the right to divorce lay entirely with the husband.

Second, the process of divorce was fatally easy. That process was founded on the passage in the Mosaic Law to which Jesus' questioners referred:

"When a man takes a wife and marries her, if then she finds no favor in his eyes because he has found some indecency in her, and he writes her a bill of divorce and puts it in her hand and sends her out of his house." The bill of divorcement was a simple, one sentence statement that the husband dismissed his wife. It is written that, "He that desires to be divorced from his wife for any cause whatsoever let him, in writing, give assurance that he will never use her as his wife any more; for by this means she may be at liberty to marry another husband." The one safeguard against the dangerous ease of the divorce process was the fact that, unless the woman was a notorious sinner, her dowry must be returned.

One of the great problems of Jewish divorce lies within the Mosaic enactment. That enactment states that a man may divorce his wife, "if she finds no favor in his eyes, because he has found some indecency in her." The question is how is the phrase some indecency to be interpreted?

On this point the Jewish rabbis were violently divided, and it was here that Jesus' questioners wished to involve Him. The school of Shammai was quite clear that a matter of indecency meant fornication, and fornication alone, and that for no other cause could a wife be put away. Let a woman be as mischievous as Jezebel, but so long as she did not commit adultery she could not be put away. On the other hand, the school of Hillel interpreted this matter of indecency in the widest possible way. They said it meant a man could divorce his wife if she spoiled his dinner, she danced, went with unbound hair, spoke to men in the streets, spoke disrespectfully of his parents in his presence, or was a brawling woman whose voice could be heard in the next house. It has been said by some that a man could divorce his wife if he found a woman whom he liked better and considered more beautiful.

The tragedy was that, as was to be expected, it was the school of Hillel whose teachings prevailed; the marriage bond was often lightly held, and divorce on the most trivial ground was sadly common. To complete the picture certain further facts must be added. It is relevant to note that under Rabbinic law divorce was compulsory for two reasons. It was compulsory for adultery. "A woman who has committed adultery must be divorced." And, divorce was compulsory for sterility. The object of marriage was the procreation of children; and if after ten years a couple was still childless divorce was compulsory. In this case the woman might remarry, but the same regulation governed the second marriage.

Two further interesting Jewish regulations in regard to divorce must be added. First, desertion was never a cause for divorce. If there was desertion, death must be proved. The only relaxation was that, whereas all other facts needed the corroboration of two witnessed in Jewish law, one witness was enough to prove the death of a partner in marriage who had vanished and not come back. Second, strangely enough, insanity was not a ground of divorce. If the wife became insane, the husband could not divorce her, for, if she was divorced, she would have no protector in her helplessness. There is a certain poignant mercy in that regulation. If the husband became insane, divorce was impossible, for in that case he was incapable of writing a bill of divorcement, and without such a bill, initiated by him, there could be no divorce.

When Jesus was asked this troubling question He was to answer it in a way which came as a staggering surprise to both parties in the dispute and which suggested a radical change in the whole situation. In effect the Pharisees were asking Jesus whether He favored the strict view of Shammai or the laxer view of Hillel and thereby sought to involve Him in controversy.

Jesus' answer was to take things back to the very beginning, back to the ideal of creation. In the beginning, He said, God created Adam and Eve, man and woman. Inevitably, in the very circumstances of the creation story, Adam and Eve were created for each other and for no one else; their union was necessarily complete and unbreakable. Now, says Jesus, these two are the pattern and the symbol of all who were to come. "Each married couple is a reproduction of Adam and Eve, and their union is therefore no less indissoluble."

The argument is quite clear. In the case of Adam and Eve divorce was not only inadvisable, it was not only wrong, it was completely impossible, for the very simple reason that there was no one else whom either of them could possibly marry. Therefore, Jesus was laying down the principle that all divorce is wrong. Thus we must note that it is not a law, it is a principle, which is a very different thing.

At once, the Pharisees saw a point of attack. Moses had said if a man wished to divorce his wife because she had found no favor in his eyes, and because of some matter of indecency in her, he could give her a bill of divorce and the marriage was dissolved. Here was the very chance that the Pharisees wanted. They could now say to Jesus, "are you saying Moses was wrong? Are you seeking to abrogate the divine law which was given to Moses? Are you setting yourself above Moses as a law giver?"

Jesus' answer was that what Moses said was not in fact a law but nothing more than a concession. Moses did not command divorce; at the best, he only permitted it in order to regulate a situation which would have become chaotically promiscuous. The Mosaic regulation was only a concession to fallen human nature. In Genesis, we have the ideal which God intended, the ideal that two people who marry should become so indissoluble one that they are one flesh. Jesus' answer was: "true, Moses permitted divorce; but that was a concession in view of a lost ideal. The ideal of marriage is to be found in the unbreakable, perfect union of Adam and Eve. That is what God meant marriage to be."

Now, what did Jesus mean? There is even a prior question, what did Jesus say? The difficulty is, and there is no escaping it, that Mark, Luke, and Matthew report the words of Jesus differently.

Matthew says:
"And I say unto you, whosoever shall put away his wife, except it be for fornication, and shall marry another, committeth adultery: and whoso marrieth her who is put away doth commit adultery."

Mark says:
"And he saith unto them, whosoever shall put away his wife, and marry another, committeth adultery against her. And if a woman shall put away her husband, and be married to another, she committeth adultery."

Luke says:
"Whosoever putteth away his wife, and marrieth another, committeth adultery: and whosoever marrieth her that is put away from her husband committeth adultery."

There is the comparatively small difficulty that Mark implies that a woman can divorce her husband, a process which, as we have seen, was not possible under Jewish law. But the explanation is that Jesus must have well known that under Gentile law a woman could divorce her husband and in that particular clause he was looking beyond the Jewish world. The great difficulty is that both Mark and Luke make the prohibition of divorce absolute; with them there are no exceptions whatsoever. But Matthew has one saving clause, divorce is permitted on the ground of adultery. In this case there is no real escape from a decision. The only possible way out would be to say that in point of fact, under Jewish law, divorce for adultery was in any event compulsory, as we have seen, and that therefore Mark and Luke did not think that they need mention it, but then so was divorce for sterility.

The greatest thing that Jesus has set before those who are willing to accept His commands is the high ideal of the married state. The Jewish ideal really gave us the basis for the Christian ideal. The Jewish term for marriage was Kiddushin. Kiddushin meant sanctification or consecration. It was used to describe something which was dedicated to God as His exclusive and peculiar possession. Anything totally surrendered to God was kiddushin. This meant that in marriage the husband was consecrated to the wife and the wife to the husband. The one became the exclusive possession of the other, as much as an offering became the exclusive possession of God. That is what

43

Jesus meant when He said that for the sake of marriage a man would leave his father and his mother and cleave to his wife, and that is what He meant when he said that man and wife became so totally one that they could be called one flesh. That was God's ideal of marriage as the old Genesis story saw it, and that is the ideal which Jesus restated. Clearly that idea has certain consequences.

This total unity means that marriage is not given for one act in life, however important that act may be, but for all. That is to say that, while sex is a supremely important part of marriage, it is not the whole of it. Any marriage entered into simply because an imperious physical desire can be satisfied in no other way is foredoomed to failure. Marriage is given, not that two people should do one thing together, but that they should do all things together.

Another way to put this is to say that marriage is the total union of two personalities. Two people can exist together in a variety of ways. One can be the dominant partner to such an extent that nothing matters but their wishes and their convenience and their aims in life, while the other is totally subservient and exists only to serve the desires and the needs of the other. Again, two people can exist in a kind of armed neutrality, where there is continuous tension and continuous opposition, and continuous collision between their wishes. Life can be one long argument, and the relationship is based at best on an uneasy compromise. Again, two people can base their relationship on a more or less resigned acceptance of each other. To all intents and purposes, while they live together, each goes their own way, and each has their own life. They share the same house but it would be an exaggeration to say that they share the same home.

Clearly none of these relationships is the ideal. The ideal is that in the marriage state two people find the completing of their personalities. Plato had a strange idea. He had a kind of legend that originally human beings were double what they are now. Because their size and strength made them arrogant, the gods cut them in halves; and real happiness comes when the two halves find each other again, and marry, and so complete each other.

Marriage should not narrow life; it should complete it. For both partners it must bring a new fullness, a new satisfaction, a new contentment into life. It is the union of two personalities in which the two complete each other. That does not mean that adjustments, and even sacrifices, do not have to be made, but it does mean that the final relationship is fuller, more joyous, more satisfying than any life in singleness could be. We could put this even more practically: marriage must be a sharing of all the circumstances of life. There is a certain danger in the delightful time of courtship. In such days it is almost inevitable that the two people will see each other at their best. These are days of glamour. They see each other in their best clothes, usually they are bent on some pleasure together, often money has not yet become a problem. But in marriage two people must see each other when they are not at their best, when they are tired and weary, when children bring the upset to a house and home that children must bring, when money is tight, and food, clothes, and bills become a problem, when moonlight and roses become the kitchen sink and walking the floor at night with a crying baby. Unless two people are prepared to face the routine of life as well as the glamour of life together, marriage will be a failure.

From this there follows one thing, which is not universally true, but which is much more likely than not to be true. Marriage is most likely to be successful after a fairly long acquaintanceship, when the two people involved really know each other's background. Marriage means constantly living together. It is perfectly possible for ingrained habits, unconscious mannerisms, and ways of upbringing to collide. The fuller the knowledge people have of each other before they decide indissolubly to link their lives together the better. This is not to deny that there can be such a thing as love at first sight, and that love can conquer all things, but the fact is that the greater mutual knowledge people have of each other the more likely they are to succeed in making their marriage what it ought to be.

All this leads us to a final practical conclusion, the basis of a relationship or a marriage is togetherness, and the basis of togetherness is nothing other than consideration. If a relationship or marriage is to succeed, the partners must always be thinking more of each other than of themselves. Selfishness is the murderer of any personal relationship, and that is truest of all when two people are bound together in marriage. The true basis of relationships and marriage is not complicated and recondite, it is simply the love which thinks more of the happiness of others than it thinks of its own, the love which is proud to serve, which is able to understand, and therefore always able to forgive. That is to say, it is the Christ-like love, which knows that in forgetting self it will find self and that in losing itself it will complete itself.

DETERMINATION TO SERVE

> *The Son of Man came not to be ministered unto, but to minister.*
> **Matthew 20:28**

Jesus said, "Yet I am among you as the One who serves." Paul's idea of service was the same as our Lord's. We somehow have the idea that a person called to the ministry is called to be different and above other people. But according to Jesus Christ, he is called to be a doormat for others, called to be their spiritual leader, but never their superior. Paul said, "I know how to be abased."

Paul's idea of service was to pour his life out to the last drop for others. Whether he received praise or blame made no difference. As long as there was one human being who did no know Jesus, Paul felt a debt of service to that person until he did come to know Him. The chief motivation behind Paul's service was not love for others but love for his Lord. If our devotion is to the cause of humanity, we will be quickly defeated and brokenhearted, since we will often be confronted with a great deal of ingratitude from other people. But if we are motivated by our love for God, no amount of ingratitude will be able to hinder us form serving one another.

Paul's understanding of how Christ had dealt with him is the secret behind his determination to serve others. No matter how badly others may have treated Paul, they could never have treated him with the same degree of spite and hatred with which he had treated Jesus Christ. Once we realize that Jesus has served us even to the depths of our meagerness, our selfishness, and our sin, nothing we encounter from others will be able to exhaust our determination to serve others for His sake.

GOD'S UNREASONABLE FAITH

Seek ye first the kingdom of God and His righteousness, and all these things shall be added unto you.
Matthew 6:33.

When we look at these words of Jesus, we immediately find them to be the most revolutionary that human ears have ever heard. "Seek first the kingdom of God." Even the most spiritually-minded of us argue the exact opposite, saying, "But I must live; I must make a certain amount of money; I must be clothed; I must be fed." The great concern of our lives is not the kingdom of God but how we are going to take care of ourselves to live. Jesus reversed the order by telling us to get the right relationship with God first, maintaining it as the primary concern of our lives, and never to place our concern on taking care of the other things of live.

"Do not worry about your life." Our Lord pointed out that from His standpoint it is absolutely unreasonable for us to be anxious, worrying about how we will live. Jesus did not say that the person who takes no thought for anything in his life is blessed; no, that person is a fool. But Jesus did teach that His disciple must make his relationship with God the dominating focus of his life and be cautiously carefree about everything else in comparison to that. Jesus is saying, "Don't make food and drink the controlling factor of your life, but be focused absolutely on God." Some people are careless about what they eat and drink, and they suffer for it; they are careless about what they wear, having no business looking the way they do; they are careless with their earthly matters, and God holds them responsible. Jesus is saying that the greatest concern of life is to place our relationship with God first and everything else second.

It is one of the most difficult, yet critical, disciplines of the Christian life to allow the Holy Spirit to bring us into absolute harmony with the teaching of Jesus in these verses.

COMMANDMENT OF LIFE

> *Be perfect, just as your Father in heaven is perfect.*
> **Matthew 5:48**

Christ tells us to be generous in our behavior toward everyone. Beware of living according to your natural affections in your spiritual life. Everyone has natural affections; some people we like and others we don't like. Yet we must never let those likes and dislikes rule our lives. If we walk in the light as He is in the light, we have fellowship with one another, even with those toward whom we have no affection.

We need to show to the other person what God has shown to us, and God will give us plenty of real life opportunities to prove whether or not we are perfect, just as your Father in heaven is perfect. Being a disciple means deliberately identifying yourself with God's interests in other people. Jesus says, "A new commandment I give to you, that you love one another; as I have loved you, that you also love one another. By this all will know that you are My disciples, if you have love for one another."

The true expression of Christian character is not in good-doing, but in God-likeness. If the Spirit of God has transformed you within, you will exhibit divine characteristics in your life, not just good human characteristics. God's life in us expresses itself as God's life, not as human life trying to be godly. The secret of a Christian's life is that the supernatural becomes natural in him as a result of the grace of God, and the experience of this becomes evident in the practical, everyday details of life, not in times of intimate fellowship with God. And when we come in contact with things that create confusion and a flurry of activity, we find to our own amazement that we have the power to stay wonderfully poised even in the center of it all.

FOCUS ON THE MESSAGE

I did not come to send peace on earth but a sword.
Matthew 10:34

Never be sympathetic with a person whose situation causes you to conclude that God is dealing harshly with him. God can be more tender than we can conceive, and every once in a while He gives us the opportunity to deal firmly with someone so that He may be viewed as the tender One. If a person cannot go to God, it is because he has something secret which he does not intend to give up; he may admit his sin but would no more give up that thing than he could fly under this own power. It is impossible to deal sympathetically with people like that. We must reach down deep in their lives to the root of the problem, which will cause hostility and resentment toward the message. People want the blessing of God, but they can't stand something that pierces right through to the heart of the matter.

If you are sensitive to God's way, your message as His servant will be merciless and insistent, cutting to the very root. Otherwise, there will be no healing. We must drive the message home so forcefully that a person cannot possibly hide, but must apply its truth. Deal with people where they are, until they begin to realize their true need. Then hold high the standard of Jesus for their lives. Their response may be, we can never be that. Then drive it home with, Jesus Christ says you must. But how can we be? You can't, unless you have a new Spirit.

There must be a sense of need created before your message is of any use. Thousands of people in this world profess to be happy without God. But if we could be truly happy and moral without Jesus, then why did He come? He came because that kind of happiness and peace is only superficial. Jesus Christ came to bring a sword through every kind of peace that is not based on a personal relationship with Himself.

Chapter VIII

A Living Principle

LIVING THE IDEAL

> *His disciples say unto him, if the case of the man be so with his wife, it is not good to marry. But he said unto them, all men cannot receive this saying, save they to whom it is given. For there are some eunuchs, which were so born from their mother's womb: and there are some eunuchs, which were made eunuchs of men: and their be eunuchs, which have made themselves eunuchs for the kingdom of heaven's sake. He that is able to receive it, let him receive it.*
>
> **Matthew 19:10-12**

When the disciples heard the ideal of marriage which Jesus set before them, they were daunted. Many a rabbinical saying would come into the mind of the disciples. The rabbis had many sayings about unhappy marriages. "Among those who will never behold the face of Gehinnom is he who has had a bad wife." Such a man is saved from hell because he has expiated his sins on earth! "Among those whose life is not life is the man who is ruled by his wife." A bad wife is like leprosy to her husband. What is the remedy? Let him divorce her and be cured of his leprosy. It was even laid down: "If a man has a bad wife, it is a religious duty to divorce her." To men who had been brought up to listen to sayings like that the uncompromising demand of Jesus was an almost frightening thing. Their reaction was that, if marriage is so final and binding a relationship and if divorce is forbidden, it is better not to marry at all, for there is no escape route, as they understood it, from an evil situation. Jesus gives two answers.

Jesus says quite clearly that not everyone can in fact accept this situation but only those to whom it has been granted do so. In other words, only the Christian can accept the Christian ethic. Only the person who has the continual help of Jesus Christ and the continual guidance of the Holy Spirit can build up the personal relationship which the ideal of marriage demands. Only by the help of Jesus Christ can we develop the sympathy, the understanding, the forgiving spirit, the considerate love, which true marriage requires. Without that help these things are impossible. The Christian ideal of marriage involves the prerequisite that the partners are Christian.

Here is a truth which goes far beyond this particular application of it. We continually hear people say, "We accept the ethics of the Sermon on the Mount, but why bother about the divinity of Jesus, His Resurrection, His risen presence, His Holy Spirit, and that kind of thing? We accept that He was a good man, and that His teaching is the highest teaching ever given. Why not leave it at that and get on with the living out of that teaching and never mind the theology?" The answer is quite simple. No one can live out Jesus Christ's teaching without Jesus Christ. And if Jesus was only a great and good man, even if He was the greatest and the best of men, then at most He is only a great example. His teaching becomes possible only in the conviction that He is not dead but present here to help us to carry it out. The teaching of Christ demands the presence of Christ; otherwise it is only an impossible, and a torturing, ideal. So, then, we have to face the fact that Christian marriage is possible only for Christians.

A eunuch is a man who is unsexed. Jesus distinguishes three classes of people. There are those who, through some physical imperfection or deformity, can never be capable of sexual intercourse. There are those who have been made eunuchs by man. This represents customs which are strange to western civilization. Quite frequently in royal palaces servants, especially those who had to do with the royal harem, were deliberately castrated. Also, quite frequently priests who served in temples were castrated; this, for instance, is true of the priests who served in the Temple of Diana in Ephesus.

Then Jesus talks about those who have made themselves eunuchs for the sake of the Kingdom of God. We must be quite clear that this is not to be taken literally. One of the tragedies of the early Church was the case of Origen. When he was young he took this text quite literally and castrated himself, although he came to see that he was in error. Clement of Alexandria comes nearer it. He says, "The true eunuch is not he who cannot, but he who will not, indulge in the pleasure of flesh." By this phrase Jesus meant those who for the sake of the Kingdom deliberately bid farewell to marriage, parenthood, and human physical love.

How can that be? It can happen that a man has to choose between some call to which he is challenged and human love. It has been said, "He travels the fastest who travels alone." A man may feel that he can do the work of some terrible slum parish only by living in circumstances in which marriage and a home are impossible. He may feel that he must accept some missionary call to a place where he cannot in conscience take a wife and begin children. He may even find that he is in love and then is offered an exacting task which the person he loves refuses to share. Then he must choose between human love and the task to which Christ calls him.

Thank God it is not often that such as choice comes to a person, but there are those who have taken upon themselves voluntarily vows of chastity, celibacy, purity, poverty, abstinence, continence. That will not be the way for the ordinary person, but the world would be a poorer place were it not for those who accept the challenge to travel alone for the sake of the work of Christ.

It would be wrong to leave this matter without some attempt to see what it actually means for the question of divorce at the present time. Remember that what Jesus laid down was a principle and not a law. To turn this saying of Jesus into a law is gravely to misunderstand it. The bible does not give us laws; it gives principles which we must prayerfully and intelligently apply to any given situation.

Of the Sabbath, the Bible says, "in it you shall not do any work." In point of fact we know that a complete cessation of work was never possible in any civilization. In an agricultural civilization cattle had still to be tended and cows had to be milked no matter what the day was. In a developed civilization certain public services must go on, or transport will stand still and water, light, and heat will not be available. In any home, especially where there are children, there has to be a certain amount of work.

A principle can never be quoted as a final law; a principle must always be applied to the individual situation. We cannot therefore settle the question of divorce simply by quoting the words of Jesus. That would be legalism; we must take the words of Jesus as a principle to apply to the individual cases as they meet us. That being so, certain truths emerge.

Beyond all doubt, the ideal is that marriage should be an indissoluble union between two people and that marriage should be entered into as a total union of two personalities, not designed to make one act possible, but designed to make all life a satisfying and mutually completing fellowship. That is the essential basis on which we must proceed.

But life is not, and never can be, a completely tidy and orderly business. Into life there is bound to come sometimes the element of the unpredictable.

Suppose, then, that two people enter into the marriage relationship; suppose
they do so with the highest hopes and the highest ideals; and then suppose
that something unaccountably goes wrong and the relationship which should
be life's greatest joy becomes hell upon earth. Suppose all available help is
called in to mend this broken and terrible situation. Suppose the doctor is
called in to deal with physical things, the psychiatrist to deal with psychological things, the priest or the minister to deal with spiritual things. Suppose
the trouble is still there; suppose one of the partners to the marriage to be so
constituted physically, mentally or spiritually that marriage is an impossibility; and suppose that discovery could not have been made until the experi-
ment itself had been made, are then these two people to be forever fettered
together in a situation which cannot do other than bring a lifetime of misery
to both?

It is extremely difficult to see how such reasoning can be called
Christian; it is extremely hard to see Jesus legalistically condemning two people to any such situation. This is not to say that divorce should be made easy,
but it is to say that when all the physical, mental, and spiritual resources have
been brought to bear on such a situation, and the situation remains incurable
and even dangerous, then the situation should be ended; and the Church, so
far from regarding people who have been involved in such a situation as
being beyond the pale, should do everything it can in strength and tender-
ness to help them. There does not seem any other way than that in which to
bring the real Spirit of Christ to bear.

But in this matter we are face to face with a most tragic situation. It often
happens that the things which wreck marriage are in fact the things which
the law cannot touch. A person in a moment of passion and failure of control
commits adultery and spends the rest of his or her life in shame and in sorrow for what he or she did. That he or she should ever repeat their sin is the
least likely thing in the world. Another person is a model of rectitude in public—to commit adultery is the last thing they would do—and yet by a day to
day sadistic cruelty, a day to day selfishness, a day to day criticism and sarcasm and mental cruelty, they make life a hell for those who live with them
and they do it with callous deliberation.

We may well remember that the sins which get into the newspapers and
the sins whose consequences are most glaringly obvious need not be in the
sight of God the greatest sins. Many a man and many a woman wreck the
marriage relationship and yet present to the outer world a front of unim-
peachable rectitude.

This whole matter is one to which we might well bring more sympathy
and less condemnation, for of all things the failure of a marriage must least
be approached in legalism and most in love. In such a case it is not a so-called

law that must be conserved; it is human heart and soul. What is wanted is that there should be prayerful care and thought before the married state is entered upon, that if a marriage is in danger of failure every possible medical, psychological, and spiritual resource should be mobilized to save it, but, that if there is something beyond the mending, the situation should be dealt with not with rigid legalism, but with understanding love.

DIVINE FELLOWSHIP

> *Then answered Peter and said unto him, behold, we have forsaken all, and followed thee; what shall we have therefore? And Jesus said unto them, verily I say unto you, that ye which have followed me, in the regeneration when the son of man shall sit in the throne of his glory, ye also shall sit upon twelve thrones, judging the twelve tribes of Israel. And every one that hath forsaken houses, or brethren, or sisters, or father, or mother, or wife, or children, or lands, for my name's sake, shall receive a hundredfold, and shall inherit everlasting life. But many that are first shall be last; and the last shall be first*
>
> **Matthew 19:27-30**

Jesus could have dismissed Peter's question with an impatient rebuke. In a sense, it was entirely the wrong question to ask. To put it bluntly, Peter was asking, "What do we get out of following you?" Jesus could well have said that anyone who followed Him in that kind of spirit had no idea what following Him meant at all. And yet it was a natural question. True, it had its implicit rebuke in the parable which followed, but Jesus did not scold Peter. He took his question, and out of it laid down three great laws of the Christian life.

It is always true that those who share Christ's campaign will share Christ's victory. In human warfare it has been too often true that the common soldiers who fought the battles were forgotten once the warfare was ended and the victory won, their usefulness past. In human warfare it has been too often true that men who fought to make a country in which heroes might live found that that same country had become a place where heroes might starve. It is not so with Jesus Christ. Those who share Christ's warfare will share Christ's triumph, and those who bear the Cross will wear the crown.

It is always true that the Christian will receive far more than they will ever give up, but what they receive is not new material possessions, but a new fellowship, human and divine. When one becomes a Christian they enter into a new human fellowship; so long as there is a Christian Church, a

Christian should never be friendless. If their Christian decision has meant they have had to give up friends, it ought also to mean they have entered into a wider circle of friendship than ever they knew before. It ought to be true that there is hardly a town or village or city anywhere where the Christian can be lonely. For where there is a church, there is a fellowship into which they have a right to enter. It may be that the Christian who is a stranger is too shy to make that entry as they ought; it may be that the Church in the place where they are a stranger has become too much of a private clique to open its arms and its doors to them. But if the Christian ideal is being realized there is no place in the world with a Christian church where the individual Christian should be friendless or lonely. Simply to be a Christian means to have entered into a fellowship which goes out to the ends of the earth.

Further, when one becomes a Christian, one enters into a new divine fellowship. He or she enters into possession of eternal life, the life which is the very life of God. From other things a Christian may be separated, but they can never be separated from the love of God in Christ Jesus their Lord. Jesus lays it down that there will be surprises in the final assessment. God's standards of judgment are not men's, if for no other reason than that God sees into the hearts of men. There is a new world to redress the balance of the old; there is eternity to adjust the misjudgments of time. And it may be that those who were humble on earth will be great in heaven, and that those who were great in this world will be humbled in the world to come.

PERSONAL PURITY

Blessed are the pure in heart, for they shall see God.
Matthew 5:8

Purity is not innocence; it is much more than that. Purity is the result of continued spiritual harmony with God. We have to grow in purity. Our life with God may be right and our inner purity unblemished, yet occasionally our outer life may become spotted and stained. God intentionally does not protect us from this possibility, because this is the way we recognize the necessity of maintaining our spiritual vision through personal purity. If the outer level of our spiritual life with God is impaired to the slightest degree, we must put everything else aside until we make it right. Remember that spiritual vision depends on our character; it is the pure in heart who see God.

God makes us pure by an act of His sovereign grace, but we still have something we must carefully watch. It is through our bodily life coming in contact with other people and other points of view that we tend to become tarnished. Not only must our inner sanctuary be kept right with God, but also the outer courts must be brought into perfect harmony with the purity God gives us through His grace. Our spiritual vision and understanding is immediately blurred when our outer court is stained. If we want to maintain personal intimacy with the Lord Jesus Christ, it will mean refusing to do or even think certain things. And some things that are acceptable for others will become unacceptable for us.

A practical approach in keeping your personal purity unblemished in your relations with other people is to begin to see them as God does. They are perfect in Christ Jesus.

STRICTEST DISCIPLINE

> *If thy right hand offends thee to sin, cut it off and cast it from thee; for it is profitable for thee that one of thy members should perish, than for your whole body to be cast into hell.*
>
> **Matthew 5:30**

Jesus did not say that everyone must cut off his right hand, but that if your right hand causes you to sin in your walk with Him, then it is better to cut it off. There are many things that are perfectly legitimate, but if you are going to concentrate on God you cannot do them. Your right hand is one of the best things you have, but Jesus says that if it hinders you in following His precepts, then cut it off. The principle taught here is the strictest discipline or lesson that ever hit humans.

When God changes you through regeneration, giving you new life through spiritual rebirth, your life initially has the characteristic of being maimed. There are a hundred and one things that you dare not do, things that would be sin for you and would be recognized as sin by those who really know you. But the unspiritual people around you will say, "What's so wrong with doing that? How absurd you are!" There has never yet been a saint who has not lived a maimed life initially. Yet it is better to enter into life maimed but lovely in God's sight than to appear lovely to man's eyes but lame to God's. At first, Jesus Christ through His Spirit has to restrain you from doing a great many things that may be perfectly right for everyone else but not right for you. Yet, see that you don't use your restrictions to criticize someone else.

The Christian life is a maimed life initially, but in verse 48 Jesus gave us the picture of a perfectly well rounded life: "You shall be perfect, just as your Father in heaven is perfect."

THE DOORWAY TO THE KINGDOM

Blessed are the poor in spirit. Matthew 5:3

Our Lord is not only a teacher. If Jesus were only a teacher, then all He could do is frustrate us by setting a standard before us that we cannot attain. What would be the point of presenting us with such a lofty ideal if we cannot possibly come close to reaching it? We would be happier if we never knew it. What good is there in telling us to be what we can never be, to be pure in heart, to do more than our duty, or to be completely devoted to God? We must know Jesus Christ as our Savior before His teaching has any meaning for us other than that of a lofty ideal which only leads to despair. But when we are born again by the Spirit of God, we know that Jesus Christ did not come only to teach; He came to make us what He teaches we should be. The redemption means that Jesus Christ can place within anyone the same nature that ruled His own life, and all the standards God gives us are based on that nature.

The teaching of the Sermon on the Mount produces a sense of despair in the natural man, exactly what Jesus means for it to do. As long as we have some self-righteous idea that we can carry out our Lord's teaching, God will allow us to continue until we expose our own ignorance by stumbling over some obstacle in our way. Only then are we willing to come to Him as paupers and receive from Him. "Blessed are the poor in spirit..." This is the first principle in the kingdom of God. The underlying foundation of Jesus Christ's kingdom is poverty, not possessions, not making decisions for Jesus, but having such a sense of absolute futility that we finally admit, "Lord, I cannot even begin to do it." Then Jesus says, "Blessed are you." This is the doorway to the kingdom, and yet it takes us so long to believe that we are actually poor. The knowledge of our own poverty is what brings us to the proper place where Jesus Christ accomplishes His work.

WITHOUT FAITH

If you have faith as a mustard seed, nothing will be impossible for you.

Matthew 17:20

We have the idea that God rewards us for our faith, and it may be so in the initial stages. But we do not earn anything through faith; faith brings us into the right relationship with God and gives Him His opportunity to work. Yet God frequently has to knock the bottom out of our experience as His saint to get us in direct contact with Himself. God wants us to understand that it is a life of faith, not a life of emotional enjoyment of His blessings. The beginning of our life of faith was very narrow and intense, centered around a small amount of experience that had as much emotion as faith in it, and it was full of light and sweetness. Then God withdrew His conscious blessings to teach us to "walk by faith." And you are worthy much more to Him now than you were in your days of conscious delight with your thrilling testimony.

Faith by its very nature must be tested and tried. And the real trial of faith is not that we find it difficult to trust God, but that God's character must be proven as trustworthy in our own minds. Faith being worked out into reality must experience times of unbroken isolation. Never confuse the trial of faith with the ordinary discipline of life, because a great deal of what we call the trail of faith is the inevitable result of being alive. Faith, as the bible teaches it, is faith in God coming against everything that contradicts Him, a faith that says, "I will remain true to God's character whatever he may do." The highest and the greatest expression of faith in the whole bible is: "Though He slay me, yet will I trust Him."

Chapter IX

The Miracle

LOST PATIENCE

> *And he saith unto them, ye shall drink indeed of my cup, and be baptized with the baptism that I am baptized with: but to sit on my right hand, and on my left, is not mine to give, but it shall be given to them for whom it is prepared of my Father. And when the ten heard it, they were moved with indignation against the two brethren. But Jesus called them unto him, and said, ye know that the princes of the Gentiles exercise dominion over them, and they that are great exercise authority upon them. But it shall not be so among you: but whosoever will be great among you, let him be your minister; and whosoever will be chief among you, let him be your servant; even as the son of man came not to be ministered unto, but to minister, and to give his life a ransom for many.*
>
> **Matthew 20:23-28**

This passage exposes the disciples. It tells that they were very ambitious. They were still thinking in terms of personal reward and personal distinction, and they were thinking of personal success without personal sacrifice. They wanted Jesus to ensure a princely life for them. Every man has to learn that true greatness lies, not in dominance, but in service, and that in every sphere the price of greatness must be paid.

But the disciples demonstrate their invincible faith in Jesus. They are thinking of a Kingdom. Even in a world in which the dark was coming down, the disciples would not abandon the conviction that the victory belonged to Jesus. In Christianity, there must always be this invincible optimism in the moment when things are conspiring to drive a man to despair. Condemning the disciple would be easy, but the faith and the loyalty which lay behind the ambition must never be forgotten.

This passage also sheds a light upon the Christian life. Jesus said that those who would share His triumph must drink His cup. What was that cup? It was to James and John that Jesus spoke. Now life treated James and John very differently. James was the first of the apostolic group to die a martyr. For him the cup was martyrdom. On the other hand, by far the greater weight of trading goes to show that John lived to a great old age in Ephesus and died a natural death when he must have been close on a hundred years old. For him the cup was the constant discipline and struggle of the Christian life throughout the years.

It is quite wrong to think that for the Christian the cup must always mean the short, sharp, bitter, agonizing struggle of martyrdom; the cup may well be the long routine of the Christian life, with all its daily sacrifice, its daily struggle, and its heartbreaks, disappointments, and tears. A Roman coin was once found with the picture of an ox on it; the ox was facing two things, an altar and a plow, and the inscription read: "Ready for either." The ox had to be ready either for the supreme moment of sacrifice on the altar or the long labor of the plow on the farm. There is no one cup for the Christian to drink. His cup may be drunk in one great moment or his cup may be drunk throughout a lifetime of Christian living. To drink the cup simply means to follow Christ wherever he may lead and to be like Him in any situation life may bring.

This passage shows us Jesus' kindness and sheds a light on Jesus. The amazing thing about Jesus is that he never lost patience and became irritated. In spite of all he had said, here were these men and their mother still chattering about posts in an earthly government and kingdom. But Christ does not explode at their obtuseness, or blaze at their blindness, or despair at their intractableness. In gentleness, in sympathy, and in love, with never an impatient word, He seeks to lead them to the truth. It shows us His honestly. He was quite clear that there was a bitter cup to be drunk and did not hesitate to say so. No man can ever claim that he began to follow Jesus under false pretenses. He never failed to tell men that, even if life ends in crown wearing, it continues in cross bearing.

The passage shows Jesus' trust in men. He never doubted that James and John would maintain their loyalty. They had their mistaken ambitions; they had their blindness; they had their wrong ideas; but He never dreamed of writing them off as bad debts. He believed they could and would drink the cup and in the end they would still be found at His side. One of the great fundamental facts to which we must hold on, even when we hate and loathe and despise ourselves, is that Jesus believes in us. The Christian is a person put upon their honor by Jesus.

SPIRIT OF MIND

> *And as they departed from Jericho, a great multitude followed him. And, behold, two blind men sitting by the way side, when they heard that Jesus passed by, cried out, saying, have mercy on us, O Lord, thou son of David. And the multitude rebuked them, because they should hold their peace: but they cried the more, saying, Have mercy on us, O Lord, thou son of David. And Jesus stood still, and called them, and said, what will ye that I shall do unto you? They say unto him, Lord, that our eyes may be opened. So Jesus had compassion on them, and touched their eyes: and immediately their eyes received sight, and they followed him.*
>
> **Matthew 20:29-34**

This is a story of two men who found their miracle. This story is significant because it paints a picture of the spirit and of the attitude of mind and heart to which the most precious gifts of God are open. These two blind men were waiting, and when their chance came they seized it with both hands. No doubt they wondered if that power might ever be exercised for them. Jesus was passing by. If they had let Him pass, their chance would have gone by forever; but when the chance came they seized it.

There are a great many things which have to be done at the moment or they will never be done. There are great many decisions which have to be made on the spot or they will never be made. The moment to act goes past; the impulse to decide fades. After Paul had preached on Mars Hill, there were those who said, "We will hear you again about this." They put it off until a more convenient time, but so often the more convenient time never comes. These two blind men were undiscouragable. The crowd commanded them to stop their shouting; they were making a nuisance of themselves. It was the custom in Palestine for a rabbi to teach as he walked along the road, and no doubt those around Jesus could not hear what Jesus was saying for this clamorous uproar. But nothing would stop the two blind men; for them it was a matter of sight or blindness, and nothing was going to keep them back.

It often happens that we are easily discouraged from seeking the presence of God. It is the person who will not be kept from Christ who in the end finds Him. These two blind men are an imperfect faith but they were determined to act on the faith they had. It was as son of David that they addressed Jesus. That meant they did believe Him to be the Messiah, but it also meant that they were thinking of Messiahship in terms of kingly and of earthly power. It was an imperfect faith but they acted on it; and Jesus accepted it.

However imperfect faith may be, if faith is there, Jesus accepts it. These two blind men were not afraid to bring a great request. They were beggars, but it was not money they asked for, it was nothing less than sight. No request is too great to bring to Jesus. These two blind men were grateful. When they had received the benefit for which they craved, they did not go away and forget; they followed Jesus.

So many people, both in things material and in things spiritual, get what they want and then forget even to say thanks. Ingratitude is the ugliest of all sins. These blind men received their sight from Jesus, and then they gave to Him their grateful loyalty. We can never repay God for what He has done for us, but we can always be grateful to Him.

RECOGNIZE JESUS

> *Peter walked on the water to go to Jesus. But when he saw that the wind was boisterous, he was afraid.*
> **Matthew 14:29-30**

Peter didn't see how high and how boisterous the wind and waves were at first. He didn't consider them at all; he simply recognized his Lord, stepped out in recognition of Him, and walked on the water. Then he began to take those things around him into account, and instantly down he went. The Lord could have enabled Peter to walk at the bottom of the waves, as well as on top of them, yet, it couldn't have been done without Peter's continuing recognition of the Lord Jesus.

We step forward with recognition of God in some things, then self-consideration enters our lives and down we go. If we are truly recognizing Jesus, we have no business being concerned about how and where He engineers our circumstances. The things surrounding us are real, but when we look at them we are immediately overwhelmed and even unable to recognize Jesus. Then comes His rebuke, "Why did you doubt?" Let your actual circumstances be what they may, but keep recognizing Jesus, maintaining complete reliance upon Him.

If you debate for even one second when God has spoken, it is all over for us. Never start to say, "Well, I wonder if He really did speak to me?" Be reckless immediately, totally unrestrained and willing to risk everything by casting your all upon Him. We do not know when His voice will come to us, but whenever the realization of God comes, even in the faintest way imaginable, be determined to recklessly abandon yourself, surrendering everything to Him. It is only through abandonment of yourself and your circumstances that we will recognize Him. We will only recognize His voice more clearly through recklessness, being willing to risk everything.

THE CONSTANT LAW OF JUDGMENT

> *With what judgment ye judge, ye will be judged; and with the measure ye use, it shall be measured to you again.*
> **Matthew 7:2**

This is the eternal law of God. It is not a haphazard theory. Whatever judgment we give will be the very way we are judged. There is a difference between retaliation and retribution. Jesus said that the basis of life is retribution: "With the measure you use, it will be measured back to you." If we have been shrewd in finding out the shortcomings of others, remember that will be exactly how we will be measured. The way you pay is the way life will pay you back. This eternal law works from God's throne down to us.

The one who criticizes another is guilty of the very same thing. God looks not only at the act itself, but also at the possibility of committing it, which He sees by looking at our hearts. We do not believe the statements of the Bible. Do we really believe the statement that says we criticize in others the very things we are guilty of ourselves? The reason we see hypocrisy, deceit, and a lack of genuineness in others is that they are all in our own hearts. The greatest characteristic of a saint is humility, as evidenced by being able to say honestly and humbly, "Yes, all those, as well as other evils, would have been exhibited in me if it were not for the grace of God. Therefore, we have no right to judge."

Jesus said, "Judge not, that you be not judged." He went on to say, in effect, "If you do judge, you will be judged in exactly the same way." Who of us would dare to stand before God and say, "My God, judge me as I have judged others"? We have judged others as sinners; if God should judge us in the same way, we would be condemned to hell. Yet God judges us on the basis of the miraculous atonement by the Cross of Christ.

Chapter X
The Power

THE POWER OF PRAYER

> *Verily I say unto you, if ye have faith, and doubt not, ye shall not only do this which is done To the fig tree, but also if ye shall say unto this mountain, be thou removed, and be thou Cast into the sea; it shall be done. And all things, whatsoever ye shall ask in prayer, Believing, ye shall receive.*
>
> **Matthew 21:21-22**

This passage of Jesus reminds us about the dynamic of prayer. If the words are misunderstood, they can bring nothing but heartbreak, but if they are correctly understood, they can bring nothing but power. Jesus states that prayer can remove mountains; if we ask in belief, we will receive. It is abundantly clear that these promises are not to be taken physically and literally. Neither Jesus Himself not anyone else ever removed a physical, geographical mountain by prayer. Moreover, many a person has prayed with passionate faith that something may happen or that something may not happen, that something may be given or that someone may be spared from death, and in the literal sense of the words those prayers have not been answered. What then is Jesus promising us through prayer?

His promise is that prayer gives us the ability to do. Prayer is never the easy way out, never simply pushing things on to God for Him to do them for us. Prayer is power. It is not asking God to do something; it is asking Him to make us able to do it ourselves. Prayer is not taking the easy way; it is the way to receive power to take the hard way. It is the channel through which comes power to tackle and remove mountains of difficulty by us with the help of God. If it were simply a method of getting things done for us, prayer would be very bad for us, for it would make us flabby, lazy, and inefficient. Prayer is the means whereby we receive power to do things for ourselves. Therefore, no one should pray and then sit and wait—they must pray and then rise and work—but they will find that, when they do, a new dynamic enters their life and that in truth with God all things are possible, and with God the impossible becomes that which can be done.

Prayer is the ability to accept, and in accepting, to transform. It is not meant to bring deliverance from a situation; it is meant to bring the ability to accept it and transform it. An example of this is when Paul desperately prayed that he might be delivered from the thorn in his flesh. He was not delivered from that situation, he was made able to accept it, and in that very situation he discovered the strength that was made perfect in his weakness and the grace which was sufficient for all things. In that strength and grace the situation was not only accepted, but also transformed into glory. Another example, when Jesus himself in Gethsemane prayed that the cup might pass from Him and He be delivered from the agonizing situation in which he found Himself, that request could not be granted, but in that prayer He found the ability to accept the situation and, in being accepted, the situation was transformed and the agony of the Cross led straight to the glory of the Resurrection. We must always remember that prayer does not bring deliverance from a situation; it brings conquest of it. Prayer is not a means of running away from a situation; it is a means whereby we may gallantly face it.

Prayer brings the ability to bear. It is natural and inevitable that, in our human need and with our human hearts and our human weakness, there should be things which we feel we cannot bear. We see some situation developing; we see some tragic happening approaching with a grim inevitability; we see some task looming ahead which is obviously going to demand more than we have to give to it. At such a time our inevitable feeling is that we cannot bear this thing. Prayer does not remove the tragedy, it does not give us escape from the situation, it does not give us exemption from the task, but it does make us able to bear the unbearable, to face the unfaceable, to pass the breaking point and not to break.

As long as we regard prayer as escape, nothing but bewildered disappointment can result, but when we regard it as the way to conquest and the divine dynamic, things happen.

INNER INVINCIBILITY

Take My yoke upon you and learn of Me. **Matthew 11:29**

Whom the Lord loves He chastens. How petty our complaining can be. Our Lord begins to bring us to the point where we can have fellowship with Him, only to hear us moan and groan, saying, "Lord, just let me be like other people!" Jesus is asking us to get beside Him and take one end of the yoke, so that we can pull together. That's why Jesus says to us, "My yoke is easy and My burden is light." You will thank God when you feel the pressure of His hand upon you.

To those who have no might, He increases strength. God comes and takes us out of our emotionalism, and then our complaining turns into a hymn of praise. The only way to know the strength of God is to take the yoke of Jesus upon us and to learn from Him.

The joy of the Lord will be your strength. If we did not know some Christians well, we might think from just observing them that they have no burdens at all to bear. But we must lift the veil from our eyes. The fact that the peace, light, and joy of God is in them is proof that a burden is there as well. The burden that God places on us squeezes the grapes in our lives and produces the wine, but most of us see only the wine and not the burden. No power on earth or in hell can conquer the Spirit of God living within the human spirit; it creates an inner invincibility.

If your life is producing only a whine, instead of the wine, then ruthlessly kick it out. It is a crime for a Christian to be weak in God's strength.

PRAY TO GOD IN SECRET

When thou pray, enter into this closet, and when thou hast shut thy door, pray to thy Father which is in secret.
Matthew 6:6

The primary thought in the area of relationships or religion is keep your eyes on God, not on people. Your motivation should not be the desire to be known as a praying person. Find an inner room in which to pray where no one even knows you are praying, shut the door, and talk to God in secret. Have no motivation other than to know your Father in heaven. It is impossible to carry on your life as a disciple without definite times of secret prayer.

When you pray, do not use vain repetitions. God does not hear us because we pray earnestly; He hears us solely on the basis of redemption. God is never impressed by our earnestness. Prayer is not simply getting things from God; that is only the most elementary kind of prayer. Prayer is coming into perfect fellowship and oneness with God. If the Son of God has been formed in us through regeneration, then He will continue to press on beyond our common sense and will change our attitude about the things for which we pray.

Everyone who asks receives. We pray religious nonsense without even involving our will, and then we say that God did not answer; but in reality we have never asked for anything. Jesus said, "You will ask what you desire." Asking means that our will must be involved. Whenever Jesus talked about prayer, He spoke with wonderful childlike simplicity. Then we respond with our critical attitude, saying, "Yes, but even Jesus said that we must ask." But remember that we have to ask things of God that are in keeping with the God whom Jesus Christ revealed.